STOP THE GOSSIPING

STOP THE GOSSIPING

IF YOU KNEW WHERE GOSSIP STEMMED

FROM . . .

YOU WOULD STOP THE GOSSIPING

MIA F. STUBBS

To order additional copies of this book, contact:

Xlibris Corporation: 1-888-795-4274: *www.Xlibris.com* **email:** *orders@Xlibris.com*

58016

CONTENTS

Special Thanks

To my Heavenly Father, whom I love so much and whom has been our True Provider, Protector, Best Friend and Confident.

I would like to thank my beautiful son, for all his support, love, complete understanding and assistance during the process of this book.

A very special thanks to all those that have contributed gossip to my life, for it has allowed this book to come forth, providing healing and encouragement for many that have been affected by gossip. A very special thanks to Jane for all her assistance with corrections of this book.

Special Message

Can you imagine allowing your only child, in whom that you love so much to die for the sins of the whole world? That through sin, mankind might live? Well that is what God sent His Only Son, Jesus to do for us. Did you know that through God's Grace and Mercy, we are here? So many times I see on the news, awful and gruesome things that people that do not know God have done to others. I then thank God for His Grace and Mercy, of keeping my mind and the mind of my son and his seed, sane. In our own sinful nature, we do not know what we would do, for the evil one would love to destroy every soul . . . but if we daily ask God for help to keep our minds strong, ask for wisdom and knowledge and protection from the evil one (satan), Our Heavenly Father will right away do it for us. God loves us so much that He sent His Son, Jesus in our place.

You may pray to Him today, and if you do not know Him, just simply say, *"Dear Jesus, I except You in my heart, please forgive me of all my sins, and I thank You for hearing my prayer, and excepting me in Your Loving Family,"* Amen.

If you already know God, will you share what God has done for you with someone else. That special someone that does not need to see or know your perfections, but your mistakes, then testimony!

Before God comes, He would like every soul to be saved, how will you contribute to this? A Good Start Is: **"Stopping the Gossip"**

Prayer of Courage

I had been in a cave, which the enemy had used people through gossip, to place me in, and I am coming out, bolder, stronger, and more powerful in My Father in Heaven. And while I am coming out, I am patting myself on the back. If it seems that I am overconfident, I apologize, that is the very result of lack of encouragement!

According to God's word, in *Proverbs 10:22, 24 "Blessings of Lord makes one rich, and He adds no sorrow with it" (24) "And the desire of the righteous will be granted"*

Tactics The Enemy Uses To Deceive Mankind:

Gossip: Rumor or talk of a personal, sensational, or intimate nature. A person who habitually spreads intimate or private rumors or facts; trivial, chatty talk or writing

Rumor: A piece of unverified information of uncertain origin usually spread by word of mouth. Unverified information received from another; hearsay

Manipulation: Shrewd or devious management, especially for one's own advantage

Mind Game: Deliberate actions of calculated psychological manipulation intended to intimidate or confuse (usually for competitive advantage)

Insinuations: An indirect or devious hint or suggestion; an indirect (and usually malicious) implication; something insinuated, especially an artfully indirect, often derogatory suggestion

Chapter 1

THE TRUE PERPETRATOR

What tool does the enemy use to implement gossip? How does he impose manipulation and insinuation? By only one way and that is through the mind. He is the seed to all confusion among mankind. He aims for his target, plants the seed of gossip in one's mind, and sits back and watches it spread like wild fire.

Since God is the only one that can read the minds of His children, we have the greatest gift of protection of our thoughts, through speaking to Him in our minds.

The enemy on the other hand, cannot read our minds. The enemy uses the tool of mind games to confuse mankind. The biggest tool that he uses through the mind is gossip.

The fall of lucifer, satan

Gossip, perpetrated by the enemy started in Heaven. Before lucifer was cast out heaven, he managed to deceive and take with him 1/3 of God's wonderfully created angelic beings. The tool used was gossip, casting rumors against our Heavenly Father.

Before creation of the earth and mankind, God created ten thousand times thousands of thousands and thousands of angels, to be His ministers. The job of the angels is to worship God all day long eternally! These perfect beings were made radiant; Our Father's powerful and beautiful light flowed to the angels giving them such powerful radiance as the sun. These perfect beings were also created to execute God's will and the will of His Son, Jesus.

According to God's word, it says in ***Colossians 1:16. Angels are God's ministers, radiant with the light ever flowing from His presence and speeding on rapid wing to execute His will. But the Son, the anointed of God, the "express image of His person," . . . "The brightness of***

His glory," . . . *"Upholding all things by the word of His power," holds supremacy over them all.*

Out of the ten thousand times thousands of thousands and thousands of angels, God created one angel head of all the other angels, his name was lucifer. And before lucifer rebelled against God, he stood before our Heavenly Creator, our Father that had created him with such beauty. This angelic being before his fall from heaven, was given the position by God, to be head of the Heavenly choir of angels. Our Heavenly Father also gave the enemy such a position of respect amongst the other angels in Heaven. With such a position given, instead of the enemy glorifying his Creator, he began to desire to glorify himself. Self indulgence, a vain heart, a corrupted spirit and his desire of wanting to be an equal to God, was the seed to him sinning. After continuous warnings that he too must worship his Creator with a grateful heart; our Heavenly Father had no choice but to remove him from heaven.

According to God's word, it states concerning lucifer in *Ezekiel 28:12-15 "Thus saith the Lord God; Thou sealest up the sum, full of wisdom, and perfect in beauty. Thou hast been in Eden the garden of God; every precious stone was thy covering . . . . Thou art the anointed cherub that covereth; and I have set thee so: thou wast upon the holy mountain of God; thou hast walked up and down in the midst of the stones of fire. Thou wast perfect in thy ways from the day that thou wast created, till iniquity was found in thee."*

God created Lucifer with perfection, so much that he began to indulge more of himself and less of our Mighty Creator that had created him. As he looked in the mirror, he became vain of himself. The vain of his beauty began to become his object along with wanting God's position and power, jealousy of the Son of God's relationship with His Father, seeded, his downfall of perfection given as a gift from our Creator. Our Creator, whom is omnipresent, reader and knower of all hearts, warned lucifer of his mind deception and the problems that could result from such evil thoughts.

In God's word it states in, *Ezekiel 28:17 "Thine heart was lifted up because of thy beauty, thou hast corrupted thy wisdom by reason of thy brightness." Isaiah 14:13,14 states, "Thou hast said in thine heart,*

. . . I will exalt my throne above the stars of God . . . . I will be like the Most High."

Gossip, Rumors Are Spread, By Lucifer

This perfect angelic being created by our Heavenly Creator; full of pride and jealousy of our Father, allowed sin to overpower his thinking, even after continuous warning. Our Father could have made him a robot, controlled his thinking and made lucifer serve Him, but our Father does not believe in forcing us to worship Him, He is a perfect Gentlemen. He desires that all of His creation worship Him because we choose to, not because He has demanded us to. This was not new to lucifer, he was very much familiar and completely understood, the true character of our overly fair Father.

Lucifer began his tactics of spreading rumors in Heaven among the other angels against God. In a powerful meeting, God met with His Son concerning the rebellious spirit of the enemy, and the results of his actions. This meeting only consisted of God and His Son, there were no angels invited. This meeting was held with the strict confidence between God and His Son. The angels all except for lucifer were at peace with any decision made by our Heavenly Creator. All the while, lucifer was outraged that he could not listen in on the meeting of God's purposes with His Son. This perfect being created by God, had been already made in charge of so much in Heaven, his greed of more overpowered him. But I must say do not feel sorry for such an evil creature, for he is the root of all pain and suffering of all mankind.

So now this once made perfect angel that has become the world's enemy, and most of all our Heavenly Father's enemy, began causing havoc, gossip, rumors against God, stating all types of untruth to the angels concerning God's character, and stating that God was not fair. The lies of gossip, from this sinful angel began impacting some of the other angels, to the point where they actually believed him, and began to side with him against God.

I can understand why God says in His word that we should not gossip, and how it angers Him so much, when He sees His creation, gossiping among one another. These actions remind Him of the enemy's behavior and the gossip he spread in Heaven. The enemy's gossip resulted in him deceiving 1/3 of the angels. Gossip was the tool used to disrupt Heavens harmony.

The root of gossip started with the enemy, in Heaven, all because of his personal jealousy. Because of lucifer's lies of gossip and rumor, one third of the angels left their Creator, God's side in Heaven, to follow him. Gossip is the root of all evil. If it caused this much chaos in Heaven, we can see how and why there is such chaos on earth. Celebrity tabloids are attempting to destroy lives with gossip. Churches are full of gossip, malicious talk against one another, cliques, members leaving the church due not feeling they fit in. The youth in schools are going through innumerable gossip, of youth wanting to fit in. The workplace is no longer an enjoyment, but employees and employers targeting one another with hurtful gossip and rumors. Marriages are torn apart, by allowing outsiders to intrude on their holy sanction, through gossip. Friendships are torn apart due to the deadly words of gossip. Most of the communities are torn apart, instead of the designed togetherness, due to prejudgment and gossip of one another.

Think about it, this is the work of satan, and how he uses gossip to separate man from one another, to maintain control over the world. This evil being knows the depression, sicknesses, suicides and destruction of mankind that can be done. If he was able to convince one third of God's perfect beings, angels, that was created sinless, having a perfect divine connection with their Creator, to leave God's side, how much more damage does he realize he can attempt to do with mankind, God's favorite creation. More examples of how the enemy used gossip, is with our original parents, Adam and Eve.

True deception of the fall of our original parents, Adam and Eve

In the beginning, when God created Adam and Eve. What tool did satan use to get Eve to disobey God, and pick from the Tree of Life, that God had warned her not to go near.

According to *Genesis 2:15-17 "And the LORD God took the man, and put him into the garden of Eden to it and to keep it. (16) And the LORD God commanded the man, dress saying, Of every tree of the garden thou mayest freely eat: (17) But of the tree of the knowledge of good and evil, thou shalt not eat of it: for in the day that thou eatest thereof thou shalt surely die."*

Genesis 3: 1 "Now the serpent was more subtle than any beast of the field which the LORD God had made. And he said unto the woman, Yea, hath God said, Ye shall not eat of every tree of the garden?"

Genesis 3:4-5 "And the serpent said unto the woman, Ye shall not surely die: (5) For God doth know that in the day ye eat thereof, then your eyes shall be opened, and ye shall be as gods, knowing good and evil."

The enemy used gossip, but in a different way to deceive Eve. There were not people that he could use to distract her from her path. Why not use gossip of the mind to deceive her. Why not gossip to her mind, to rebel against God, her Creator, as he has already done with 1/3 of the angels that was removed from Heaven along with him. Though God had already warned Eve not to touch or eat of the Tree of Life, satan, came as a beautiful talking crafty serpent to deceive Eve. Eve caught up in the beauty of the talking serpent, listen to lies and gossip of satan. In satan's deception, he gossiped about God, stating that if both Eve and Adam was to eat of the Tree of Life, that their eyes would be open to see what God sees, and have the knowledge that God has.

Instead of Eve rejecting such gossip spoken against the One that created her and Adam, she listened and became more intrigued by the chatty, deceiving enemy, which resulted in her sinning. I am sure when she stood listening to the talking serpent that she thought of it being no harm, but that she is actually gaining knowledge about important information that was purposely left out for her benefit.

Isn't that how most feel today, when listening to or reading juicy gossip about the life of someone else. Thinking that it is completely innocent, and that it cannot hurt to listen, or read for a moment. But this is a deception! This untruth or truth belongs to life of someone else, and they are due the same privacy that the one listening or reading would want to have. Just imagine yourself being the center of gossip, or being read about.

The enemy has perpetrated gossip, so much to the point where it is unrecognizable that he is the true root of any hurtful chaos. Centuries of experience in perpetrating gossip has given him the advantage of hiding his place of manipulation. Gossip starts with one person, and then spreads, well this one person is him. If he was able to deceive our first earthly mother through gossip of mind, just being created in perfection, how much more does he think that he can do with us today?

Rumors, gossip, has been so watered down over a long period of time by the enemy that people do not even think of its effects in ruining lives, and most do not even consider it a sin in God's Eyes. Many others knows that it is a sin, but think that compared to other sins, that it is very small or it does not really count in God's Eye; but this is a huge deception, for in God's Eye, if you have committed one sin, you have committed them all.

The enemy deceived through gossip to Adam and Eve Seed . . .

The enemy did not just gossip, rumor against God to create the fall of our first mankind, Adam and Eve. After Adam and Eve was removed from the Garden of Eden, because of their disobedience, the enemy decided to deceive, cast confusion, gossip, rumor, plant seeds in the mind of one of their children, Cain. *Genesis 4:1-2 "And Adam knew Eve his wife; and she conceived, and bare Cain, and said, I have gotten a man from the LORD. (2) And she again bares his brother Abel. And Abel was a keeper of sheep, but Cain was a tiller of the ground."*

The enemy, through gossip of the mind, insinuation to produce jealousy caused Cain to kill his brother Abel. The enemy convinced Cain, that God loved Abel more then He loved his brother. Strong manipulation through mind games, the enemy was able to convince Cain to delete his brother from the face of the earth. Cain was then cursed by God for the death of his brother, which increased the curse of the earth where mankind's offspring would be bored. These tactics, working towards the plan of the enemy, in destroying God's work of art, mankind and nature.

The enemy, crafty and a behind the scenes perpetrator of gossip, had already accomplish his goal of deceiving God's first creation of mankind, Adam and Eve, through gossip. There was no way that he could stop there, he decided if it was so easy for him to deceive Eve through gossip, and cause her and Adam both to be kicked out of the Garden of Edom, why not now target their children as well. Surely if he was able to master such deception through gossip of God's first mankind creation, at their strongest mental sharpness, he thought, he definitely would be able through this same deception of gossip, to deceive Eve's seed.

God created Adam and Eve, in complete perfection; their mental thought capacity surpassed any earthly gray haired genius of mankind. They both were created first on God's manufacturer line of perfection for mankind. Both were not boggled by worries, stress or any distractions that could distort their thinking or cloud their minds. They used a 100% of their thinking capacity given as a gift to them from God.

Even, with both having such perfect minds, not created in sin, but complete perfection, they were still somehow able to be deceived through gossip against their Creator, God, by the enemy. The wise and very crafty enemy attempted to laugh at God, that His creation of the first of mankind, that He loved so much had now also disappointed Him. But before you weep for Our Father, realize that He is so All-Powerful and loving, that He could have destroyed the enemy in a blink of an eye, for how he deceived His first creation of mankind.

However, God was disappointed in His creations disobedience, and lack of not listening to His warnings, He unfortunately dealt with Adam and Eve's sin by removing them from the Garden of Edom. Even in His disappointment, as a loving and true Parent, He still provided for them.

In Genesis 3:21-24, "Unto Adam also and to his wife did the LORD God make coats of skins, and clothed them. 22 And the LORD God said, Behold, the man is become as one of us, to know good and evil: and now, lest he put forth his hand, and take also of the tree of life, and eat, and live forever: 23 Therefore the LORD God sent him forth from the garden of Eden, to till the ground from whence he was taken.

24 So he drove out the man; and he placed at the east of the garden of Eden Cherubims, and a flaming sword which turned every way, to keep the way of the tree of life.

Though Adam and Eve sinned by disobeying God, He loved them still so much, though He was disappointed with their sin. Our Heavenly Father saw the invisible strings planted by the enemy to destroy His creations.

And even still in His mercy and grace provided for Adam and Eve, and had a complete plan for their lives and their children's lives for salvation.

This luxury the enemy does not have. There is nothing the enemy can ever do to regain God's love, once he was removed from Heaven; all ties were broken between Our Heavenly Father and him. The enemy knows that he will never have a chance as mankind has, of God's forgiveness and salvation. This infuriates him and this is why he continuously makes it a point to get mankind, God's creation, off their designated path, through the mind game deception of gossip.

Now the enemy has already targeted Eve through the deception of gossip against Our Creator, and since he has accomplish this task, he decides why not plot another target through gossip. Adam and Eve were born in God's perfection. In the enemy's deception, he has concluded if he was able to deceive Eve and Adam in perfection, why not try to deceive their seed that will be born in sin. Mankind today is the seed of our first earthly mother and father, Adam and Eve.

The enemy has continued centuries later to gossip to the mind of many individuals. This tool he uses to create depression, sicknesses, chaos and confusion among mankind. If he was able to deceive through gossip of the mind our earthly parents, Adam and Eve, when they made perfect using 100% of their God given thinking capacity, how much does he try to create such gossip of mankind's mind today!

Every deception, temptation in the bible, was attributed to some type of mind game insinuated by the enemy to destroy mankind. How was all of this done, through gossip and manipulation of mankind's mind? Now it has been established that the enemy started havoc in Heaven through gossip against Our Creator toward his angelic creations, and caused one third of the angels to fall and be removed from Heaven. The enemy then used gossip, manipulation of the mind, to Eve, when she touched and ate of the fruit God warned her not to partake of.

All this was to lead to his desire of decreasing the quality and quantity of God's creation. God's creation, mankind's existence was measured by centuries. Meaning the life span was till 950 + years old. God created mankind with powerful wisdom and rare powers and abilities. Our Father created mankind as giants of great stature and strength, and with very powerful discerning gifts in devising evil. The enemy knew that if this wonderfully given gift from God to mankind was in anyway tampered with, through mind distraction, separation and disobedience of Our Creator, that it would weaken the strength of mankind. This is where the enemy uses gossip, manipulation of the mind, to confuse the path of mankind that has been designed by Our Heavenly Father.

The enemy wanted to confuse the mind of mankind through distracting them away from God, by centering their love on themselves and their own needs (self love), worship of foreign idols, proud hearts, and ignorance of their special gifts in God. These are the very things that separated the enemy from God, resulting in him being thrown out of Heaven. The enemy determined that he would distract mankind from God in the same way he tempted himself. The enemy in no way is ignorant of his powers, but yet he insists through gossip of the mind to attempt to keep mankind ignorant of their God given powers. This evil manipulator knows that if mankind was to grasp the full concept of our inherited power in God, that he would be defeated, and outnumbered.

Genesis chapters 6 and 7, tells how the enemy had corrupted mankind's mind so much through gossip and manipulation of the mind, against God; that God, in return sent a prophet, Noah, to warn mankind of how their actions were corrupt and unacceptable. Noah was instructed by God to build an ark of a specific dimension that would be used as protection for his family. The building of this ark, with all its dimensions could have very well fit each listening soul, if they would comply with the warnings of God. The corruption and sin among the earth had spread so, that God had sent a warning through Noah, that the earth He once created for mankind to enjoy would be destroyed by flood, if they did not change from their sinful ways and turn back to Him.

"By faith Noah, being warned of God of things not seen as yet, moved with fear, prepared an ark to the saving of his house; . . . and became heir of the righteousness which is by faith." (Hebrews 11:7) Noah was laughed at and gossiped about concerning his message of warnings that mankind should repent of their sins, turn from their wicked ways, and turn back toward their Creator. It took Noah one hundred and twenty years to build the ark. The enemy had not just tormented mankind to disobey God for centuries after creation of Adam and Eve our first earthly parents, but

for one hundred and twenty years he manipulated many to self indulged in every sin that could be done. All of this was completed through gossip of the mind, deception, manipulation of the mind, to turn from God, and to not listen to His prophet, Noah. Mankind had lost morals and values of God's Laws, but followed their own man-made laws.

Imagine this, that God could have warned through Noah, for a mere week, for mankind to change their stubborn hearts, but being a gracious, loving and a merciful God, He extended the time for mankind for one hundred and twenty years. Our loving Creator, pleaded through His prophet, for mankind to change, for them to recognize the evil tactics of the enemy attempting to turn their hearts further away from Him.

Genesis 6:9, 11,13 states, "These are the generations of Noah: Noah was a just man and perfect in his generations, and Noah walked with God . . .[11] the earth also was corrupt before God, and the earth was filled with violence.[13] And God said unto Noah, The end of all flesh is come before me; for the earth is filled with violence through them; and, behold, I will destroy them with the earth."

Though Noah continually was the center of ridicule, was gossiped about, and called a deluded old man, he continued with building the ark, in preparation for him and his family, and anyone willing to listen to the warnings from God. Noah was mocked and laughed at, called all types of names, to discourage his spirit, to stop building the ark; but he never faltered in completing his assignment. He also followed the plan of God by continuing to warn the people, in spite of the horrendous things said against his character.

I am sure that it took great courage to continue building the ark, though there had never been any signs of rain, nor flood. Being gossiped about that he was losing his mind, rumors that he must be a false prophet, among other imaginable things said against him, I am sure had to hurt. Though his character was being degraded by the mere one's that he was told to warn, it still took a great amount of courage. I am sure that at some point, he too begin wondering, if it was really worth it; would God ever back him up to send some type of sign that would confirm His warnings. But strong in his belief, he kept his head high, even amongst the gossip and rumors concerning his character. Out of his fear of God, he held close to God's truth and trusted what God told him to do.

After one hundred and twenty years of ridicule, rumors and mockery of his character, warning as God told him, his hard work of measuring, gathering and building the ark, and most of all God's mercy, grace and love stretched beyond limit, God sent the flood.

We must ask ourselves, how long will God warn us about hurting one another with our words through gossip? Though many may feel that gossip in God's Eye is a small sin, it is a sin, and there is no greater or lesser sin in His Eyes. God states in His word, that we should not gossip, cast rumors amongst our brethren. Anything that will separate members from the church, affect youth in the schools, rob one of one's character, affect employees in the workplace, assist in tearing apart marriages, separate communities, could this be not more evident that this is the work of the enemy to rule the world. In God's word *Exodus 23:1 "You shall not circulate a false report. Do not put your hand with the wicked to be unrighteous wicked." Proverbs 25:18 states, "A man who bear false witness against his neighbor, is like a club, a sword and a sharp arrow." Psalms 34:13 states, "Keep your tongue from evil and your lips from speaking deceit." And in Psalms 57:4 states, "My soul is among lions, I lie among the sons of man who are set on fire, whose teeth are spears and arrows, and their tongue a sharp sword."*

Even after all of this, the enemy is still on his task of destroying God's creation, mankind, through gossip and manipulation. Now it has been established that the enemy used gossip of the mind to manipulate God's crowned creation, mankind. And as a result of complete wickedness and disobedience, not taking heed to the warnings for one and twenty years sent by His prophet Noah, that Our Creator sent a flood upon the earth, to cleanse the earth of all evil the enemy had committed. Our Creator spared the life of Noah and his family as a result of his obedience in building the ark, and following the instructions of God. *Genesis 7:1 "And the LORD said unto Noah, Come thou and all thy house into the ark; for thee have I seen righteous before me in this generation."*

Though, the prophet, Noah was very grateful of God's mercy to him and his family; among his family he had three sons; the enemy begins once again of planting the seeds of gossip of the mind. Noah had three sons named: Shem, Ham and Japheth. There were to be founders of the human race. Mankind, (though our original parents being Adam and Eve) due to the flood would now be birthed through their family lines. The enemy did not want to see peace, beauty and purity in the earth. Moving without delayed he began creating havoc amongst the only family saved by God in the flood. Outside of our first earthly parent Adam and Eve, Noah and all of his family were the first inhabitants of the earth after the flood. Our first parents had been deceived through gossip of the mind to disobey God, why should the enemy not try again with now the new inhabitants of God's earth.

Noah's son, Ham and all his seed thereafter were deceived greatly for centuries by the enemy with gossip of the mind. The enemy convinced through gossip of the mind, heavy manipulation to turn against God. Noah's other sons, respected their earthly father, Noah. Shem and Japheth, reverence and obedience to God manifested a long line of blessing for them and their seed.

The enemy has seemed to manipulate sin through gossip of the mind toward Noah's son, Ham and his seed. Unfortunately instead of possessing a grateful spirit that their lives had been spared in the horrible flood, they lacked reverence of God, they blamed God, and turn to the worship of foreign idols. This work was the work of the enemy, Ham and his seed was blinded by traps of their enslavement of the enemy. One would think after watching and listening to the warnings of his father, Noah for one hundred and twenty years to repent and to take heed to God's warning would also recognize the enemy at work to destroy mankind. All of these done by the enemy through of the gossip of the mind, resulting in manipulation of the minds with thousands multiplied to rebel against God.

The bible is full of stories where the enemy manipulated God's children through gossip of the mind. Here are examples, just to name a few, of how the enemy used false insinuations; individual gossip of the mind; the spread of gossip among many of God's chosen, to ruin the character:

> ✓ *In Genesis, chapters 15-18 God told Abraham, he would be the father of many nations. That his wife Sarah shall bear a son, even in her old age. The enemy gossiped to the mind of Sarah that surely God must be mistaken, for she was too old to have a child;* the enemy also tried to gossip to the mind of Abraham, that the promises of God, that he would be the father of many nations, would never take place. Every soul today are the seed of Abraham.

- ✓ *Exodus chapter 1-4* Moses feared going before Pharaoh to free the Israelites. The enemy gossiped to the mind of Moses, insinuating fear in his heart that Pharaoh would have him killed for requesting such a command. The enemy also manipulated gossip of the mind by trying to convince Moses that he did not have a voice that could be respected or heard, among Pharaoh, in leading the Israelites into the Promise Land.

- ✓ *Exodus chapter 15-18* The Israelites after being freed by God, and led by Moses from the bondage of Pharaoh, in their flight of victory, the enemy through gossip of the mind, manipulated them into believing that, their freedom of hard times, and entering into the Promise Land would not take place, and that their fate was to die without food and water. They began to complain to Moses, that their life as slaves to the system of Pharaoh would be better than trusting in the system of God to supply all their needs.

- ✓ *Judges chapters 13-16* In the story of Samson. God had given Samson the gift of physical strength. God requested, for the wealth of Samson's strength to be maintained, that he must not share the fact of his hair being the key to his strength. And he was not to intermingle or intermarry with the worldly women, idol worshipers. The enemy through gossip if the mind, insinuated to Samson, that his strength was so powerful, and wisdom strong enough that he would never allow himself to be tricked by the women of the world. This overconfident spirit led to his temporary separation from God and being tricked by the enemy through Delilah. God had already warned him to stay away from such worldly women. Samson temporary love for Delilah had a stronger weight then the fear and love he was suppose to have for God.

- ✓ *1 Samuel chapters 1-2* The story of Hannah and the gift of her son, Samuel. Hanna was in deep depression that she was childless. The enemy harassed her spirit, through gossip of the mind, that she would never have a child. The enemy convinces Hannah through manipulations and continued insinuations of mind gossip that the reason she was childless, was because God was displeased with her, and that she would never have a child. God granted her the request of a son, his name being called Samuel. Samuel was favored by God, and used at a very young age, for the work of God.

- ✓ *1 Samuel chapter 16* David and Goliath. The enemy used Goliath, a huge giant to terrorize the Israelites for a long period of time.

David highly favored in God, and a strong believer in the power of God. Spoke in the Name of Our Creator, that he would slew Goliath and free the Israelites of their continued terror; the enemy was imposing on them through Goliath. The enemy attempted gossip of the mind through fearful manipulation, by telling David in his spirit and through his family and friends, that he was not capable of winning such a battle. His faith was so strong in God that it was through God; he killed Goliath in victory, and freed the Israelites from continually being enslaved to Goliath.

✓ *Matthew chapter 1* The birth of Jesus was an exciting time for Mary and Joseph and most of all Our Heavenly Father. When the angel appeared to Mary in a dream, and told her that God would impregnate her with a son, and that she should name Him, Jesus, for He shall die for all the sins of mankind. The message given to Mary by the angel from God was not share with the whole village, only with Mary and then Joseph. Mary being known as a virgin, engaged and now pregnant, made room for assumption for those in her village. Those in her village were used by the enemy to cast rumors, gossip against Mary. She knew what the angel of the Lord had told her and Joseph concerning the birth of Jesus, in a dream. The angel told Mary, that Jesus would be born through the true power of His Heavenly Father, God.

The enemy thought if he was to stress Mary out with gossip of the mind, and use the people in her village to cast such hurtful rumors toward her, that such stress could cause complications in her pregnancy. The enemy hoped that he could prevent the birth of Jesus from happening. It was the enemy's goal through gossip and rumors to discourage the hearts of Mary and Joseph. Carrying the burden of gossip in their village, was intended by the enemy to be so overwhelming for the couple that if placed under such pressure it might cause damage to God's Divine and Appointed Son, our Savior. This inflicted hurt, in the enemy's warped way of thinking could possibly result in our Savior not being born. The world, then, would be without a Divine Holy Savior and mankind would be left in his hands and used as his playground.

✓ *Matthew 4:1-11* The enemy tried to tempt Jesus in the wilderness. The enemy tried to gossip of the mind with Jesus in the wilderness.

Jesus had been without food or water, for forty days and forty nights. Our Savior had been without sleep, and though the Son of God was born perfect and sinless, He still was born in human flesh. He endured all temptations that mankind face daily, but He never sinned. The enemy attempted to tempt Jesus with gossip of the mind, when he felt He was at His weakest point. The enemy attempted to unsuccessfully get Jesus to focus more on physical food, rather than the true spiritual from God. Asking Jesus to turn the stone to bread, at His weakest moment after not eating for forty days and forty nights; this only shows His true selfish and cunning character of always attempting to tempt through gossip of the mind at our weakest moments.

The enemy's gossip of the mind through manipulation could not tempt Jesus. Jesus knew that He was an Example for mankind, and as our Example, His sacrifice in weakness, would be a reminder to mankind of our strength in His Father. Jesus knew for centuries the enemy had tempted mankind through gossip of the mind, and it was most important that mankind was to have the perfect example of how to resist the enemy, at our weakest or strongest times.

This task was not easy for Jesus, all the weight He would bear for the world through His death and then resurrection, hungry, thirsty and tired. But His love for His Father's will and His love for mankind were most important to Him; to teach mankind how to be victorious over the enemy. The enemy attempted to tempt Jesus, while in hunger, by saying, *"If You are the Son of God, command that these stones become bread."* Each time the enemy attempted to tempt Jesus, He quickly responded with authority! *"Man shall not live by bread alone, but by every word that proceeds from the mouth of God."*

The enemy fled when Jesus spoke in authority. But he returned again to Jesus, attempting to tempt through mind manipulation (gossip of the mind) to test the power of Jesus. It was evil to attempt to manipulate Jesus' mind while He is yet tired, hungry, thirsty and bearing the weight of the world on His shoulders was evil, *"If You are the Son of Man, throw Yourself down, For it is*

25

written: He shall give His angels charge over thee, in their hands they shall bear You up, lest You dash Your feet." Jesus responded quickly with, *"It is written you shall not tempt the Lord your God."* The enemy knew that Jesus is the Son of God, for it was this cunning liar that had used his gossip tactics to spread rumors against Jesus. The enemy thought his plot of mind manipulation of Jesus, would cause Jesus to want to prove His authenticity to him. Jesus knew this, and even in weakness, rebuked him, through the word of God.

Jesus did not have to be born as a baby, for He already existed and lived in Heaven with God. He left His palace and place with God, to come down to earth, to save all of mankind from death. Jesus did not have to die for mankind, but for the sake of the world because of gossip of the mind, then sin, all being imposed by the enemy; our Precious Jesus with strong love ransomed His life. Mankind needed a Savior, a Representative, One powerful enough even in human flesh to reclaim what the enemy once attempted to take from mankind; victory in God, and dominion over the earth.

The enemy, feeling he had the upper hand due to Jesus being without sleep, food and water, attempted to gossip of the mind through insinuations that He has left His home in Heaven, to now be living on earth without a place to lay His head. The enemy attempted to insinuate that he is now ruler over earth, and Jesus was on his turf, and that if He was to worship him, he would give Jesus ownership of all the earth. How could the enemy give something that does not belong to Him? Dominion over the earth was given to mankind by God. Jesus the Son of God had come to claim back for mankind what had been given by His Father. There was not one need that His Father, our Creator, would not supply for Him, if He asked. For what belonged to the Father, also belonged to the Son.

The enemy attempted to tempt Jesus by saying, *"All these things I will give You, if You fall down and worship me."* Jesus responded with authority by saying, *"Satan! For it is written, you shall worship the Lord your God, and Him only you shall serve."* The enemy fled from Jesus; his evil tactics against Jesus were defeated by with His words of authority. Jesus is our example how to resist the enemy through temptation today.

Our Savior redeeming mankind of death through His blood was the greatest love that a Heavenly Father and Son could give. The enemy had used many to cast gossip, rumors against Jesus. The enemy had used those that Jesus had come to save; give life through His death, to be the same ones to beat, spit and cause immeasurable pain and anguish to a Savior sent here to conquer life, through His death. The enemy had caused such hatred and anger amongst the people against Jesus, till the true purpose of why He unselfishly came, was forgotten.

Many had forgotten the miracles Jesus had performed, the sermons He had taught, the love that He showed to the rich and the poor. Our Savior was beaten and scorned all day and night. The enemy right there to urge such evil to be committed upon our Savior, insisted on insinuating to the mind of our Savior, that His Father did not love Him. That a Father would never allow Him to be beaten, mistreated and put to death for people that were sending him to His death. The enemy had gossip to the mind of Jesus during His years on earth that He would be dying for mankind that did not appreciate what He would be doing for them. Our Savior's selfless act is a result of true unconditional love for mankind. Though He was innocent, but treated as a criminal He never complained, never said a word in His own defense, but, *"Father, forgive them, for they know not what they do."* He did not have to speak a word, His action of unconditional love was all the evidence mankind needed.

God created earth and mankind with splendor, beauty and all of perfection. Driving on the highway this morning, passing the trees that are damaged and cut down, they lack the natural beauty once given by Our Creator in love for mankind. It was Our Creator's desire for earth to be the paradise for man. If mankind would not sin, we would live in perfect harmony with Him, forever. Our Creator spoiled mankind with the gift in creation of earth; beautiful clouds, the sun, moon and stars, nature and much more. He did not hold back in showing such love He had for us in creating earth.

Though the enemy has corrupted the earth, trying his best to delete it and mankind of its natural beauty, it has been God that is still in control. Our Creator in His infinite mercy and grace has not given us over to the enemy, even with all of our imperfections and sin. He knows the invisible strings that are being dangled by the enemy to actually lash out against Him, so He keeps warning us in many ways, as He warned in the days of Noah, to repent and follow Him.

The enemy has tried for century after century to taint the beauty in God's creation. With all the sicknesses, depression, drugs and murder; all these things the enemy has used mankind to take part of; it is not an actual target to us, but a direct result of his hatred toward God. Since we are God's creation, we are caught in the middle. Our Creator knowing this keeps giving us ways to be victorious in each and every one of our circumstances. It is His will that we are victorious in Him, and the enemy each time is defeated.

Now that many have been exposed to the truth of where gossip stems from, and how for centuries, the enemy has used gossip of the mind to be his source of controlling mankind. It is our responsibility to adhere to what God says in His word concerning gossip being a sin, and run far away from taking part in gossiping against one another. **For gossiping against one another, destroying the character of our brethren does not glorify God, it glorifies the enemy!**

Now that it has been made evident who the true perpetrator of gossip is, we must not continue to be enslaved in the hurtful and evil tactics of the enemy to turn mankind against one another. This very act goes against the Law of Government for earth to work in harmony together with one another. *2 Chronicles 7:14 "If my people, which are called by my name, shall humble themselves, and pray, and seek my face, and turn from their wicked ways; then will I hear from heaven, and will forgive their sin, and will heal their land."(KJV)*

"Now That You Know Where Gossip Have Stemmed From . . .

You Must . . . Stop The Gossiping!"

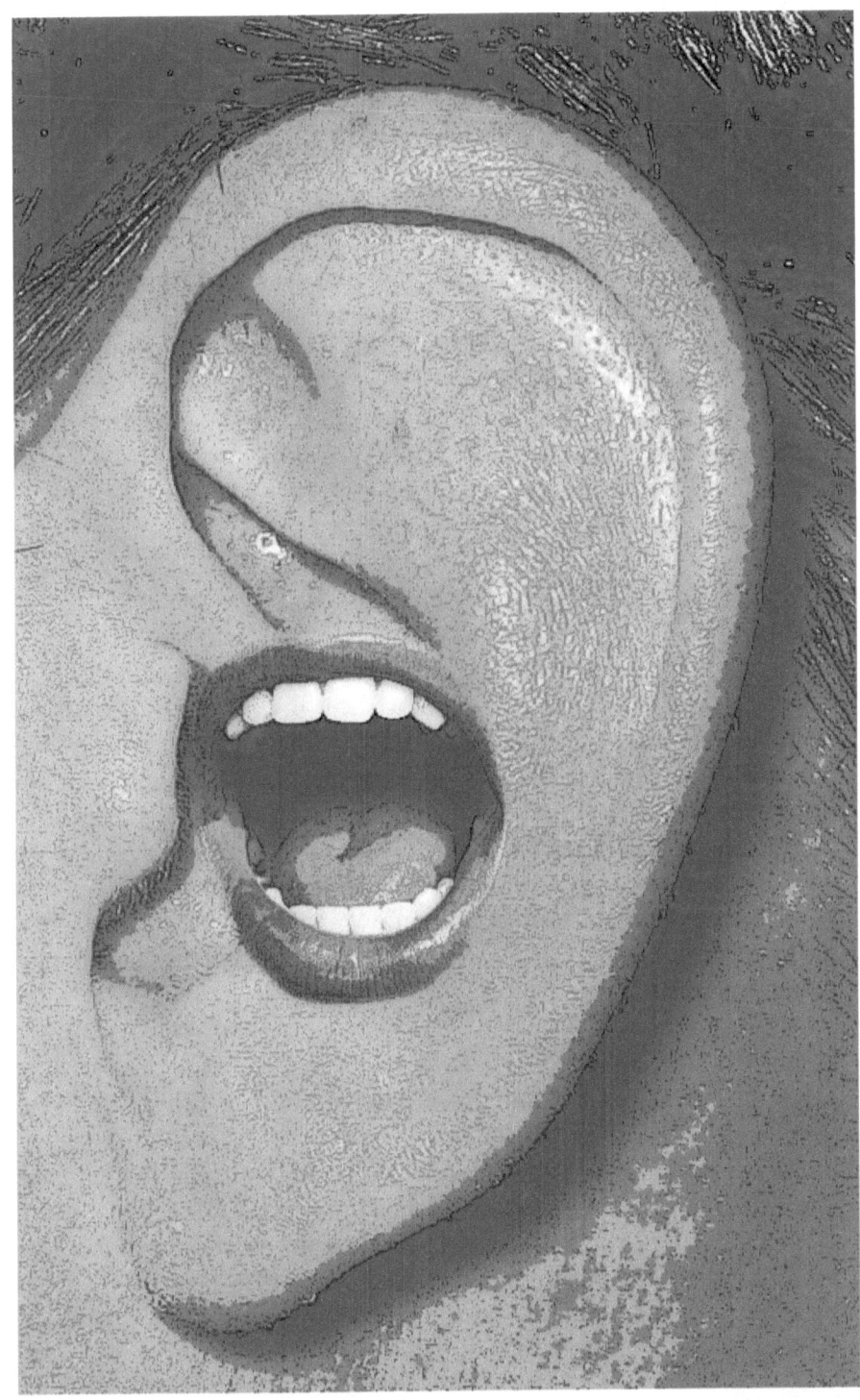

Chapter 2

GOSSIPING AFFECTS . . . INDIVIDUALS

Ruins of gossip of individuals, has been a problem for a long period of time. The enemy meant to humiliate and hurt our Precious Jesus, through the gossip of those that were attacking His character and His origin from God. Being so in love with us, He knew He had to be the perfect Example. His focus being powerfully connected to His Father and His destined path could not be broken. Our Precious, Jesus, born in human flesh, tempted, rejected and betrayed by those that claimed they loved Him and those that did not; never gave any weight to the attacks of the enemy, but remained perfect without sin.

Anytime one of us faces any type of gossip, we can freely go to Jesus, our Intercessor to our Father to unleash our burden. Individuals like me that have faced or are facing gossip; I would like you to know that I understand that it hurts. Most individuals that participate or initiate gossip do not understand how hurtful it is, and how the affects of gossip can be deadly when targeted. They feel that the one facing gossip should be stronger, and brush the affects that gossip leaves, off of their shoulders. Someone very unkindly told, me that I needed to build a bridge and cross over it. Unfortunately, it was a sad time when I needed encouragement of one that could comfort me with kind words; I had already had a full dose of harsh words said against me, and more or less needed a listening ear, not judgment in how strong I should be.

This is how I am able to relate to others that feel this way to. Most of all God can relates to all of His children, mankind. There is nothing that we experience that He had not yet experience. In John 1:1-2, states: *"In the beginning was the Word, and the Word was with God, and the Word was God (2). The same was in the beginning with God*. Meaning though God, being Creator of the all of Heavens and earth, angels, the enemy, mankind and all things, humbled Himself to be mistreated, so that we would be comforted and He be a Example of comfort through His word.

The characteristics of gossip and gossip itself have stemmed from the enemy. These tools of gossip are used through bullying, mind manipulation, false insinuations, jealousy, trouble making and seeking, a liar, thief of one's character, a mind and heart wrecker. These are just a few of the characteristics of the enemy. Those that inflict gossip on others do not clearly understand that they are being used by the enemy.

Most people like me that have been a victim of gossip, rumors; are categorized by people and this is why they are gossiped about. The one's causing the most damage through their verbal insinuations, are categorizing the personalities of those they gossip against, because their actions do not calculate to their standards. Our Creator in all His power created even the snowflakes none being alike. There are no handprint or fingerprint the same. The purpose is, God loves originality; it shows in all of nature. He loves color that is why He created mankind with such beautiful shades of colors. Animals in variety and all of nature. God could have made everything and everyone robots, all the same, but this would have been very boring for our Creator.

Being a victim of gossip, does not mean you are unaware of what is being said about you, or who is gossiping against you. It also does not mean you are afraid. Speaking from my own experience, I chose not to give others that had intentionally hurt me, the satisfaction of my response. On the other hand, confrontation, for me, was a chain of individuals that are caught up in he said, she said, each denying their involvement in their attempts to ruin mine and other's character.

If you are a victim of gossip, though it hurts, I would like for you to remember one important thing; people only talk about people that they are intimidated by, that they see greatness in, the ones they potentially think of as a threat. This act was done through the enemy to Jesus by those that He loved unconditionally. The enemy has always been in fear of Jesus and all power possessed by Him and His Father. In this same way, because mankind is the creation of God, the enemy is intimidated by mankind. We have something that he wished he could have; a Savior that died for us, so that we may live and a Father and Creator that unconditionally loves us forever. The enemy lost every chance of that when he continuously rebelled against God. And for centuries through gossip, have attempted to destroy the lives of God's creations. Of course, his attempts are voided out as a blank check by God.

If you are a victim of gossip, just know, you have now been told that you are truly special by the one that gossiped about you. Everything that they have said to destroy your character was the opposite in their mind of what they truly feel of your character. If those like me that have been hurt through gossip, would exercise our power more, instead of the feelings of being hurt, we would send those that have gossiped, as crying babies to their crib. Our presence is bold and powerful, and with a continual pat on the back whether from ourselves or someone that truly cares, our inner spirits will heal the broken pieces inside once broken through the affects of gossip.

Driving in my car, I began talking to Jesus in my spirit about how gossip had hurt me so much in the past. My efforts of always over giving, feeling this was the only way I had to earn a position in God's family. Always contributing words of encouragement to another soul's spirit, but not always receiving that same encouragement in return. I think my desire of always wanting to help someone else, or even put a smile on someone else face, was my way of saying, "Ok God, am I now good enough to be a part Your family?" I was not always made to believe or encouraged in my spirit, by some followers of Christ, that I was good enough.

Well, Jesus responded in my spirit. He told me, first and foremost, I was a part of His family, and not only I, but my son, He loved him a whole lot, and he too is a strong part of His family. And that also do not worry about being a people pleaser, it can be very exhausting. That, yes He loves the things that I am trying to do to get His attention, and to please Him, but that I already have His attention, and have had it from the time I was born. That the seeds I sow now will benefit not only my son and his future, but his seed as well.

And last of all, if I am ever feeling misunderstood, misused and unappreciated, He truly could relate; He then shared these feelings with me: For on a greater scale that I could not ever imagine, He too, was misunderstood, misused and unappreciated for the gift He gave to all mankind, His life! In my spirit He shared that He left His position in Heaven, next to His Father, to come to earth to be a Savior for a lost race, He loves so much, and though He could have made a place for

Himself, He humbly did not always have a place to sleep at night while on earth. That though He always had His Father and angels to talk with, and receive encouragement from, He did not have a earthly friend that sticketh closer than a brother. That even though His disciples, He called His friends loved Him, yet some of them betrayed Him. Also even though He had healed the sick, and created many miracles, many of these same people assisted in crucifying Him. That with sadness but great love for man, on the night before His crucifixion, no man can conceive how He was terrorized by His enemies, those He came to die for. He was hated by many but loved by few. How no man will ever be able to conceive the weight of the world that was on His shoulders, but that He knew through His death, mankind would have life and receive victory over the enemy. And last of all, with all of this, He still asked for the sake of all mankind, **"Father forgive them, for they know not what they do!"**

He also let me know that He knew that the enemy had hurt me through gossip in the past and so many others as well. But that He is aware of it, and will bless me because of it, and for me to keep moving forward, and to help those along the way, but most of all, ask Him for help to help myself, so that through my testimony many would be comforted.

For all the victims of gossip, rumors, bullying, mind manipulation, false insinuations, may your life and mine be enriched! May God replace our ashes with beauty! May our joy be increased three fold!

Throughout this book, I would like to share with you articles of great comfort:

Our Enemies Are Our Footstool . . .

Article by: Mia F. Stubbs

In life when you are wronged by someone, God says your reward is in Heaven, but you also receive a taste of it on earth.

Our favor that we receive in life, which is circumstantial, according to the blessing promised by our Father, is payment from God, for going through something for His Namesake. God has promised when we go through something for Him, He owes us and He pays all His debts on time.

If our enemies only knew, each time, that they had been influenced to hurt us, that they actually set us up in a position to receive a huge blessing, that we were not suppose to receive, they would always be kind to us!

Thank God for friends and enemies and all the contributions they make in our lives.

GOSSIP . . .

"HOW NEGATIVE ACTIONS AND CONVERSATIONS AFFECT OTHERS . . . ."

Article by: Mia F. Stubbs

Read Exodus 23:1

"You shall not circulate a false report. Do not put your hand with the wicked to be an unrighteous wicked."

How do we look at the people we work with, assemble at church with, or even go to school with? Do we look at people through the eyes of what others portray that person to be, or through our own eyes? A co-worker told me, he stores in the back of his mind what is told to him, and then observes that person when talking with them. I thought to myself that storing someone else's thoughts of another person just gives an eventual crack for doubt of the person down the road.

It takes one individual, to demolish a person's name, and it unfortunately takes that person that it has happens to a long time of discomfort to repair it. Personally experiencing gossip, has allowed me to reach out to others that are too experiencing the effects of gossip. I believe that God will use it to make a change for others that are experiencing it too and start the process of putting an end to it. To man it seems that it may be impossible, but with "God all things are possible". Whenever I see someone that seems to be unfriendly, or someone that seems to be hurt inside, I am very empathetic to ask myself what is it that I can do to encourage that person. If someone comes to you and start gossiping about one of the students at school, or in church if the members are talking about the homeless man that has walked in or even at work, if a group of people are talking about one the employees or employers, you can walk away, it takes a real woman or a real man to speak out against it or close their ears to it, to start making a strong difference.

A good way to put a stop to gossip is to imagine each time that you are talking to someone that God is standing right next to you.

Proverbs 25:18

"A man who bear false witness against his neighbor, is like a club, a sword and a sharp arrow."

Psalms 34:13

"Keep your tongue from evil, and your lips from speaking deceit."

Psalms 57:4

"My soul is among lions, I lie among the sons of men who are set on fire, whose teeth are spears and arrows, and their tongue a sharp sword."

Prayer: Dear God, please help us to be cautious of our words, help us to speak words that build up, not tear down, in Jesus Name, Amen

Thought For The Day*: A good way to put a stop to gossip, is to imagine each time that you are talking with someone that God is standing right next to you!*

GOSSIP AFFECTS . . . THE WORKPLACE

Gossip in the workplace has also been happening for centuries. The enemy has disguised gossip to point where it is undetectable. Being an employee of a local automotive assembly plant, and of course being made one of the targets of gossip while working there, pushed me to leaving my position and job. I have prepared a small business model of how gossip creates a negative environment; also how lack of employee/ employer trust, teamwork and communication affects the productivity due to it distracting the employees.

Optimistic Atmosphere:

- Happy employees, produce a continued positive atmosphere
- A continued positive atmosphere, produces a continued safe environment and increased production
- Increased production will lead to increased sales, greater job opportunities and job security

What Is The Current Problem?

- Gossip, rumors among employees, employee cliques
- Employee distractions due to depression and stress
- Lack of communication, motivation and teamwork
- Tardiness, easily distracted, missing work due to problems in the workplace

The Result in Work Performance Due To These Problems:

- Employee not working to their full potential
- Production delayed, numerous errors
- Lost focus, sleeping on the job

- Employees are a huge part of the wealth of any organization when an employee efforts are not recognized, it could lead to "I Don't Care Attitude" which can hugely affect the company
- Company sales are hugely decreased, layoff's, job security threatened
- Decreased job benefits, decreased medical insurance
- Businesses closed due to high loss of sales, unhappy clientele due to high production errors, more money is being paid out for production errors rather than profit
- Business owners, partnered corporations, board members have lost what they have worked so hard at building

What Needs To Be Done?

- Stop or reduce gossip through problem solving
- Team effort and brainstorming and recognition of employee efforts
- Increased enthusiasm through positive actions and communication
- Increasing employee participation and allow their concerns to be voiced and their concerns to be recognized
- Teamwork surveys that allows employees to give feedback on all positive changes and it's affects
- Providing departmental committee mediators for employees with conflict issues
- Instead of group cliques of gossip, have group cliques of prayer for increased productivity, for that is the greatest reward for any company's success

The Workplace Result:

- Peace, stress free environment in the workplace, decreased tardiness, and employees taking off from work
- Enjoyable atmosphere, positive attitudes, alertness on job
- Each employee will give a 100%, desiring to see daily success, and most of all will not work in fear, but will work their position as if it is their personal business
- Increased production and productivity, increased sales
- Customer/client satisfaction and referrals
- Competitors wanting to duplicate success

- Increase the wealth of communities by supplying job employment opportunities
- Most of all through prayer cliques, God is invited to sanctify the environment, for the wealth of the company

Our Jobs Are Our Stepping Stones . . .

Article by: Mia F. Stubbs

My experience as being an employee, so many times I would see other employees coming to work with a look of punishment. The job no longer had a meaning purpose, but considered a trap to care for their families.

One thing I realize, our jobs are not meant to imprison us till retirement, but to be used as our stepping stones toward early retirement; to observe, plan, and then utilize toward our goal of success. Our jobs teach us how to perform success in our own business with basic steps we learned while we were there.

Everyone is born to lead and not to follow.

The difference between a rich man and a poor man is the steps that he took . . .

Life Experiences Allows Us A Huge Access . . .

Article By: Mia F. Stubbs

Certified? Or have a degree? Worked hard in accomplishing your goals in life? What a accomplishment for weathering your educational storms. I would like to dedicate this to anyone that has never been recognized for weathering the storms of life that has prevented furthering their education; sacrificing your dreams to provide for your family, lack of positive influence in your life, or even life turns choking you to the point where you are not able to believe in yourself. You have something so great to offer others, and that is your experiences in life. Sharing your pain can be warning or a comfort to another. A lot of the times we don't share our pain because we feel no one would understand, we feel embarrassed, or we bury it, but without sharing we could be preventing the growth of another.

Counsel yourself through counseling another, that is an automatic free degree and the rewards are from the school of TRIUMPHANCY!

THE EFFECTS OF GOSSIP . . . THE CHURCH

Proverbs 18:8 "The words of a gossip are swallowed greedily, and they go down into a person's innermost being."

1 Corinthians 12:27 "Now ye are the body of Christ, and members in particular."

Gossip is such a huge problem in the church. And most followers of God do not realize the affects that gossip has on new believers coming to Christ, and those that have been members of the body of Christ. The church does not realize that gossip is the root of evil endorsed by the enemy. Most members feel that gossip is considered a small sin in God's Eyes, with that being said the sin of gossip is mostly overlooked. Lack of knowledge of how the enemy uses gossip to destroy the body of Christ, can result in many souls leaving the church with the feelings that God condones this type of behavior. In no way does Our Creator whom knows where gossip has stemmed from, which is the enemy, take pleasure in being misrepresented, by those called and used to carry out His task of increasing His family.

In the beginning of this book, it is evident of who the true perpetrator of gossip is, and how for centuries he has used gossip to distract many of God's children off their path. The enemy has used gossip of the mind, using others to carry out his dirty work of discouraging the heart and soul of God's creation, mankind. The church, members of the body of Christ, in a sincere effort to keep the laws of Christ, in some way neglect one of the many most important laws of God's government, which is gossip, trivial chatter.

Every church desires to increase the family of Christ, and in this effort, they tend to miss the hurting soul in need of the great attention of a Savior.

The hurting soul that does not know God, or has not completely formed a personal relationship with God, needs the nourishment of the church to assist them through prayer and the feelings of being welcomed into God's family.

John 3:16 "For God so loved the world, that he gave his only begotten Son, that whosoever believeth in him should not perish, but have everlasting life." God sent His Son, Jesus to die for all sinners. It is an insult to our Savior when the body of Christ; the church, cast gossip, make judgment against those really in need of the help of God. A question is asked when members of the body of Christ are categorizing groups of people, have church cliques, spreading rumors, passing judgment against one another, is this action glorifying God or is it partnering up with the enemy. The church is a hospital for everyone from the pastor to the congregation. Each person coming into God's dwelling has a specific prayer need whether similar or dissimilar. Instead, rumors of gossip are being spread among the church members glorifying the enemy and reducing the power that God would like to release to each needed soul. The lock of hands in prayer of support for one another, love and confidence needs to be accomplished, to block the enemy from being the blessing blocker.

So many adults and youth's image of God has been marred by what they seen and heard said, among members of the body of Christ. The feeling of not being accepted for who they, and who they can become as a member of the body of Christ, is not edified and nourished. This truly disappoints God and is in disrespect to the Only Son, He sent to die for those that are lost. God sent His Son, to be a Precious Lamb for sinners. Who does the body of Christ, think are sinners? Well, it is those in the world and those in the church, for there is no man perfect, but God, and His Son. This is the biggest deception the enemy uses to stop new members from joining as members of the body of Christ. This deception is done, by making those members of the body of Christ to believe that there are no imperfections amongst them, to look down on and gossip concerning others imperfections. This only weakens the desire of those looking and wanting a Savior, due to them feeling they could never amount up to becoming what God envisioned them to be, an included part of His family. This most of all is a misrepresentation of Whom God really is, a Savior and Lover for all of mankind.

Ephesians 4:12 "For the perfecting of the saints, for the work of the ministry, for the edifying of the body of Christ." There are many hurt souls that are touch by God through a sermon or an encouraging word told to them. Mankind can not in any way read the motives on one's heart, only God. Participating in casting rumors, gossip against them, can do more damage than good. It can give the impression to that soul, that God is the same as the gossiper and are quickly turn off, not wanting to have anything to do with God. And the enemy knows this, for this is the tool he uses to remove man from coming to Christ. How do you know when God is drawing a soul to Him? We do not know, that is why it is most important that we do not allow the enemy's tactic of gossip to be the tool used, to discourage that soul from coming forth.

When Jesus left His palace in Heaven to come down to earth, Him being our perfect example of how we are to live and love unconditionally, catered to the poor in heart and spirit. Him being our perfect Example, leaving riches and honor in Heaven, did not surround Himself or praise those that did not need Him, only those souls that did. Are the church members of His body giving praise to those that are the best dress, most talented singers, and the most popular? Or are they joining together with those gifted by God to help others low in spirit in need of the nourishment to know what their special gifts are.

1 Corinthians 12:12 "For as the body is one, and hath many members, and all the members of that one body, being many, are one body: so also is Christ." Our Creator in designing mankind gave each a special gift to add to body of the Christ to strengthen the body of Christ for the betterment of increasing the body of the Christ. The enemy knows that when all of mankind joined together with such powerful gifts given by God, that he would be outnumbered, his evil tactics would not work, but would be very evident. So he endeavors to create chaos through cliques, rumors, gossip, separation, members and nonmembers with feelings of being left out. The enemy believes and knows the power of God, and that it can only be release when there is harmony and peace, so he creates havoc amongst one another, and once again he attempts in such indiscreet sneakiness to use God's creation, mankind to carry out his plan.

How many people have been sent on a mission from God to a church, and then have been misjudged, gossiped about, felt uncomfortable or even unwelcome, and have left that church, sometimes never to return again. We must recognize that this is how the enemy breaks the cycle for the end process. That end process can consist, of many of God's children on a mission to save many souls through sharing their testimonies. They are depending on the full body of Christ, to assist in building their spiritual gifts. Undernourished or not properly receiving the proper spiritual food, can result in them feeling they are not competent or strong enough to complete another of God's greatest task, and gives up, leaving the tasks given by God, undone. The enemy in returns loves that fact that he has stopped the process of bringing more souls to Christ, through the many assigned to do their part into bringing more souls to God for salvation; for this is one less person he will burn for at the end.

The weakest and the one most considered to be the biggest sinner, is the one God also loves to use, for then this is how He is glorified through their testimony. God says, *"That harvest is plenty and the laborers are few."* The enemy has hurt so many people, many that have joined the church or already members of a church, but there is an even larger amount in the world, that has been hurt. If there is an overwhelming amount of gossip, non-support, judging, pointing the finger among the body of Christ, how can God send the really hurt one's in from the world, that need to really know about the love of God. Everyone is need of a Savior; the Savior is not the members of the body of Christ. The members of the body of Christ are the nourishing tool to point those in true need, to God, this includes the body as a whole.

I pray for change for the churches, for gossip to be completely deleted, for this is the weapon of the enemy. I pray also that all are able to look at one another in love, it does not matter who you are, what you've done, or where you've been, through the Eyes of God, but all are made to feel the warm welcome of being in God's family. When that task is done, we then will see the true hurt of many, through the Eyes of God, and most of all, who the true perpetrator of their hurt is, the enemy.

Leviticus 19:16 "Thou shalt not go up and down as a talebearer among thy people: neither shalt thou stand against the blood of thy neighbor; I am the LORD."

Psalms 41:6 "And if he come to see me, he speaketh vanity: his heart gathereth iniquity to itself; when he goeth abroad, he telleth it."

Ezekial 36:3 "Therefore prophesy and say, Thus saith the Lord GOD; Because they have made you desolate, and swallowed you up on every side, that ye might be a possession unto the residue of the heathen, and ye are taken up in the lips of talkers, and are an infamy of the people."

1 Timothy 5:13 "And withal they learn to be idle, wandering about from house to house; and not only idle, but tattlers also and busybodies, speaking things which they ought not."

Proverbs 26:20 "Where no wood is, there the fire goeth out: so where there is no talebearer, the strife ceaseth."

2 Corinthians 12:20 "For I fear, lest, when I come, I shall not find you such as I would, and that I shall be found unto you such as ye would not: lest there be debates, envyings, wraths, strifes, backbitings, whisperings, swellings, tumults."

Lord~ . . . . Increase Our Church . . .

Article By: Mia F. Stubbs

In God's dwelling, the pastor and the church are praying for increase. God says, "The Harvest is plenty and the laborers are few."

In church service, one morning a prostitute and a drug dealer, dressed not up to the standards of those that are judging, walks in the door. They are rejected and gossiped about by the members of God's dwelling; they leave, never to return to that church.

Next week service, the pastor and the church prays again for increase for the church.

God responds by showing, He sent the increase through the prostitute and drug dealer. God was going to increase the church through them. Through them, He was going to bring thousands off the streets that are lost.

God is a mysterious God; He sends unexpected packages to accomplish His Greatest Tasks . . . so then He Will Be Glorified!

Who Are Between The Stationed Churches...

Article By: Mia F. Stubbs

Why is it that people are not attending church? There are lots of churches, but a world full of people that are few, entering in. So much pain and suffering, economy issues, people are looking for a Savior. As a result of not really not knowing how to find Him, they are going to Tarry Card Readers, Psychic Readers, and even into Horoscopes, to find out their destiny and powerful gifts.

In my experience and observance, many people looking for a Savior are felling to go inside of the churches, in fear that they may not be accepted. The members of the church on the inside may appear to them to be of such a high Christian standard, that immediately those on the outside needing and wanting to come in, feel they would never be able to measure up to the standards of those they are observing and decide it is easier to wait till they can get themselves better.

This is very disappointing to God, for none of us can ever rescue ourselves from our own circumstances; the church is a hospital for everyone from the pastor to the congregation and any of those in need of a family. A lot of times many forget what rock God rescued them from, when He called them to become a part of His family. When we share these testimonies with others it secures a bridge for the one listening to walk over to. It also shows our imperfections. We are all sinners, most of all when we neglect to share our testimony with others of how God has rescued us, it becomes an insult to Him, the True and Loving One that died for our sins~

Keeping it real, remembering where we were in life when God let us know that we are proudly His children, should never be forgotten, but used as a prayer of THANKFULNESS to Him and in that thankfulness, it should be made our duty to increase His Family by sharing when and how He saved us!

GOSSIP AFFECTS . . . YOUTH IN SCHOOLS . . .

Psalms 144:12 "That our sons may be as plants grown up in their youth; that our daughters may be as corner stones, polished after the similitude of a palace."

Mentor, Train, Equip, Release . . .

Gossip is a huge problem in the schools. Parents do not realize in talking on the phone; when company is over, that their chatty harmless conversations about someone else child, gives the child secretly listening the thought that gossip is harmless as well. It is beyond me, how a parent can gossip concerning someone else's child, but forget yet that they too are parents, and would not want anything to be said concerning their child.

In the bathroom, I heard two ladies discussing a child that attends the schools where their children attended. One parent began saying, "She is such a troubled child, poor thing, her future will not amount to much, she doesn't even have friends." The other parent in response said, "I know, there is no help for her." As I am listening, I knew that God, too, is also listening, and must be thinking, "Ladies, do you know that I am standing right here, why you are not speaking blessings over this young lady's life?" What was even more surprising that they did not fear the fact that they too are parents in need of God's covering over their children? Every parent loves to speak confidence concerning their child's efforts, and achievements with others. And that is good, confidence in your child, and letting them know you have spoken confidently concerning their efforts, is very encouraging for them. It is most discouraging when a parent is boasting concerning a child, while casting rumors or gossip concerning someone else child, for whatever reason they decide is the basis of their belief or delusional belief.

The enemy has used gossip to affect so many youth in the schools. The tools of gossip the enemy uses, are through peer pressure of wanting to fit in, stress, jealousy, bullying, premarital sex, alcoholism, drug use, being influenced to want to be like or look like those on the magazines and television programs. The enemy knows that the youth today, will be the wealth of the world tomorrow. The enemy fears that when properly nourished, armored with scriptures, possessing the testimonies of adult warriors in God, knowledge of past and present mistakes of many followers of God, knowledge of spiritual gifts through nurturing, continuous prayer and supplication, the youth of our world today combined together with wisdom and knowledge, standing strong in prayer, would powerful be his defeat. As he has for centuries, attempted to attack the minds of mankind through gossip of the mind, he attempts to try to keep the youth ignorant of such powerful gifts that have been given by God.

The enemy would like to have the youth of today, through gossip of the mind, as little children in a candy store of many flavors and colors. This hater of mankind, attempts to dangle eye candy before the youth through: models on magazines covers, young ladies feeling they have try diet pills, bulimia and anorexia, plastic surgeries to change their mirrored image given to them by God. The enemy thinks in his cunning way that diet pills could possibly lead to another pill, eventual attempting to push them into becoming an addict. Young ladies wanting to be models are being tricked by perverted individuals under the influence of the enemy through being told they must participate in premarital sex acts as a trade off to become a celebrity.

The youth men of today are dazzled by the lyrics of raps, with such strong violence and profanity. Lacking the wealth of male role models or even a father figure in their life. (Young men, you are blessed as well as the young ladies). But I must share with you how the enemy would like to attempt to blind them with eye candy. They desire for riches and fame, to buy the biggest house, all the latest clothing, jewelry, the attention of young women, a quick fix of being in the control seat. In this same way the enemy tempted Jesus in the wilderness. Matthew 4:9, the enemy says to Jesus, *"And saith unto him, All these things will I give thee, if thou wilt fall down and worship me.* Jesus rebuked the enemy quickly by saying, *". . . Get thee hence, Satan: for it is written, Thou shalt worship the Lord thy God, and him only shalt thou serve."* It was the desire of the enemy to promise the wealth of the world to Jesus, if He would bow down and worship him. Jesus rebuked the enemy right away. Dominion, ownership of the earth was given to mankind as a gift from God. How is it that the enemy can promise Jesus something that He and His Father gave to mankind, as a gift? These are deceptions of the enemy. God has given us the gift of dominion over the earth, but in order for this to be obtained, you have to go to the answer key, the bible, to claim what has been rightfully given to you. Ask God to show you what He would like you to have, to glorify Him through helping others, and He is more than willing to hear your prayer and answer it.

Youth, please understand, this cannot be stressed enough, Jesus, Our perfect Example, your Savior, wanted you to not be ignorant of the cunning tactics of the enemy. Jesus says, *"You are to be wise as a serpent, and harmless as a dove!"* Meaning be on guard at all times, fully spiritually armored, the serpent was the evil device used by the enemy to trap Eve, your first earthly parent. Stay connected, reconnect or get connected with God, He is your only true tool and source. He will fight all battles for you, and allow you to see how the enemy was trying to deceive you.

The enemy is attempting to become bolder with his tactics. At one time, fads were just a change of a clothing styles and hair. The enemy is attempting to use the fads of eye candy today to be such as, stress of wanting to fit in, premarital sex, drug use, alcoholism, violent dominance in dating relationships, and committing a variety of violent acts, self infliction, rebellion, disobeying laws and authority figures, disrespect to their parents, mentors, elders and all those over them, the bad boy and girl mentality. This is why Jesus came as our personal Savior and Example of how to live, and how to rebuke the enemy right away through his indirect temptations. The enemy attempts to destroy and harden the mind, the body and the soul. The enemy does all these through gossip of the mind.

On the flip side, youth for centuries have been taught to respect their elders, leaders, those in higher positions. But seeing so much of the imperfections of leaders, elders of the church, the imperfections of those in high position; can create a stumbling block (NO WEAPON FORMED, YOUTH!). It has been the enemy's purpose to have it, where now, the youth do not know in whom to trust or even respect, in a world of such chaos. How can a youth respect and honor God, when God has not been feared through those that are His representatives. How can youth respect the laws of government, when they see those in authority of the laws is not keeping the laws themselves. This is how the enemy uses the gossip of the mind toward the youth to want to go their own way. God in return, steps in, for His love is great for the little ones, to save them. The most effective gift to be given to youth today, is resources, shared wisdom and knowledge of those that gone before them, experiences of life.

God, our Designer, Creator of the life of mankind has the only capability of reading our minds and searching the hearts of man. The enemy on the other has no ability to read minds as our Creator. The method he uses is gossip of the mind through manipulation and false insinuations. Just as the enemy was able to discern, in the beginning of creation with our first earthly mother, Eve, her thoughts and curiosity to tempt her, through studying her body language. In this same way he attempts to discern the thoughts and curiosity of our youth today, as he has done throughout history.

The enemy being an invisible evil spirit that can take on the likeness of anything or anyone with breath, has thousands of deceptive disguises. Imagine a invisible spirit that watches and studies the body language of mankind all day long, to try to discover the weaknesses of that individual. This is how the enemy then uses gossip of the mind, to deceive the mind through the body language he has observed. We should be so thankful to God, for not allowing the enemy to have his way with mankind, but in His tender love, mercy and grace; He keeps His powerful protection all round the minds, body and soul of the youth today, if they allow Him to. God being the Ultimate Parent does not want us or His special babies, the youth, to be ignorant of devices of the enemy, but wants them to be on guard of how the enemy works, so that his temptations do not entrap them!

Romans 8:38-39 "For I am persuaded, that neither death, nor life, nor angels, nor principalities, nor powers, nor things present, nor things to come, nor height, nor depth, nor any other creature, shall be able to separate us from the love of God, which is in Christ Jesus our Lord."

Youth of today, need to be equipped with the victories of all adults as well as their failures. They need to be in touch with every experience that every adult has gone through; this is how knowledge is gained. So many times parents, teachers, pastors, priests, family members, and all others will not share their past or personal experiences to contribute positivity for youth's growth. There is great wealth in learning from others failures and victories. It teaches how to duplicate victory from a past victory experiences, it also teaches how to duplicate victory from a past failure experiences. The enemy does not want the youth today to be exposed to this knowledge; this would enable victory.

So he attempts to keep adults feeling that they do not want to share their experiences. Parents keep quiet of their past, due to not wanting their children to know the same silly mistakes they make, were similar to same ones they made in their younger years. If they had only shared this from the beginning, this would prevent their child from repeating the same mistake. Teachers are teaching how to succeed through proper education and focus, but still they lack to share the many errors they too have made, most of all, remembering how they felt, when they too were students. The pastors are the shepherds used by God to lead; it is of great importance that their testimony of how God brought them from where they were to where they are now is shared. The youth needs the strong spiritual food from those pastors and elders of the church that are sincere and strong in the Lord, to assist in edifying their spiritual gifts given by God. God does not look upon man for where they are now, only where they are going. Youth need adults to not judge them by their physical make-up, but by their ability and willingness of wanting to try. And for those that do not feel they want to try, they must be nourished with much love to heal the invisible wounds the enemy has inflicted through various circumstances.

Prayer is the strongest gift that adults can give to youth. Prayer for blessings over their lives, not just their own child, but someone else's child as well. Gossip and prejudgment can bring stress and low self esteem to anyone. Remembering that the words that come out of any adult's mouth, concerning someone else's child through hurtful gossip, can easily be remedied by putting your foot in the other parent's or youth's shoe.

Youth today, I like to share with you that I am a parent of a wonderful son; I have made many mistakes, and have faced many challenges in the past, but in learning and still learning from my mistakes; I have been able to share a wealth of wisdom concerning my mistakes, failures and victories, as a learning guide to assist in his growth. If there is ever a time, you should know this in your spirit, it is now! If and when anyone tells you can't, know that **"you can"** a step further, **You WILL!** You will **have victory in Jesus! Stay focus! Listen to the wisdom** of those that care about you, **stay closely connected to God**, for **He is your Deliverer and Protector and the only One that provides His favor** in your life, and uses **your enemies to be your stepping stones**. *"No weapon formed against your life shall prosper, and every tongue that rises up against you, shall be condemned, all these in Jesus Name!"*

For Those That Agree, May God Enrich Your Life!

The "M" Is Your True Origin . . .

Article By: Mia F. Stubbs

Do you know Whom you have originated from? There are so many abandoned children and even adults today, never knowing their true origin. Unfortunate circumstances of one may appear that they have been left without a trace of family to love them.

If you would take a moment to look at your hand, in the center is a stamp from God. This stamp is designed and engrained in our hand, so that we would never have to question our True Origin, God.

For many that feel they are here without a purpose, a parent, any family to love you, I ask that you look always at the center letter "M" stamped on your inside your hand. This "M" stamped inside your hand is confirmation from God of your origin, and all of our origin.

Just as a child when they are born, they might have their mother's eyes and fathers smile, or have some type of physical similarity to their parent.

God our, True and Thee Ultimate Father whom loves us so much, made us all, in His likeness and He stamped us all before we came out of our earthly mother's womb, with the letter "M" so that we would always know our True Origin is from Him, and the real meaning of that "M" means "Mine"~

Youth Reference help Index: (Gossip Affects: Youth in School)

Paperboi Ministries: An prayer group for youth that are facing adversity, providing encouragement, inspirational music, and most of all a listening ear.

Visit: *www.stopthegossiping.com*

Bullycide of America: Advise for youth that are being bullied at school, or in the neighborhood.
Visit: *www.bullycide.org*

Free Crisis Hotline: Open 24 hours a day 365 days per year. Call with any problems, anytime!
Visit: *www.BoysTown.org*

Children Hotline: Free family counseling services. Crisis hotline.
Visit: *www.sfcapc.org*

Youth Education Programs: Educational Programs for low income students. Learn more and get involved.
Visit: *www.BreakthroughCollaborative.org*

GOSSIP AFFECTS . . . CELEBRITIES

Most believe that when you become a celebrity, the problems of life no longer exist. The enemy wants many to believe that the earthly riches are the only remedy for happiness. The gossip of the mind manipulator wants to dazzle the eyes of many souls watching celebrities on television and readings in the magazines that this is the ultimate dream to accomplish. Being in the lime light, just allows the enemy to magnify what he feels are their imperfections. These imperfections are normal problems that many of the worlds face, but because celebrities are in the lime light, the enemy uses it to be magnified on a larger scale. So many celebrities have been affected by gossip through television programs and magazine covers. Privacy of the lives has been altered with constant press and paparazzi flooding their every move. This can be among other stresses, a huge pressure. Each move made is being considered a role modeled example for all of their fans. From receiving traffic tickets to various accusations, whether true or false is magnified to the limited.

Many celebrities are not exempt from the enemy tactics. The enemy plays the gossip of the mind with them as well. They have to deal with the day to day issues, of wondering in whom to trust, their physical appearance, among other temptations. I feel sad for celebrity's whose lives, whether truth or untruth are made to be visible for entertainment of others to read or watch on television. I feel that a lot of the time, people like to read or watch on TV, what they feel is juicy gossip concerning someone else's life. It gives some, the satisfaction of, for that moment of forgetting the problems that might be happening in their own lives, to focus on someone else's problem. In most cases, reading or watching someone else's life or character being demolished, makes the reader and watcher feel as if they are not the only one going through life's discomfort. The only problem, the celebrity's life being ridiculed has been made the subject of entertainment. It is evident that the enemy has taken a sin, this sin hated by God, and has made many believe this is another form of entertainment.

The enemy targets them with the same stresses of life as anyone else. Lies, gossip anyway to ruin their character is a way of sending them into depression and feelings of being alone. The enemy uses magazines, television, and word of mouth to send hurtful gossip, rumors to expose the life of celebrities with all types of accusations, whether true or false. Unfortunately all the unselfish and good deeds done and contributions made are not exposed to show the true heart of their character. A good example is MC Hammer, a man with a good heart, whom is not honored in his unselfish giving. Other celebrities that have been ridiculed about how they are dealing with the terrible pressure the media have unfairly placed on them. Other celebrities that have gone to other countries to adopt children of other races outside of their own race, to provide a better life for them, an opportunity that might not ever been made available for that child or their family. It is a good thing that God knows His children, and knows their heart and motives, and sends blessings according to those good deeds done in secret or in public.

The enemy is the excuser that always wants to set up trouble, and then expose it, to destroy the character of the target. It is he that does not want the good of one's character, and unselfish contributions to be exposed, for such good character represents the character of God, and his job is to try to destroy the character of God and all of God's creation. But do not worry, God is aware of all matters, and fights all battles, victory is always ours!

So many other celebrities have given so much, and instead of placing their kind efforts on the front of the magazines; rumors, gossip, destructive articles are exposed in its place, all in which no one knows whether it is true or untrue, but that celebrity accused.

What a shame when gossip is used to be entertainment for its readers, listeners, watchers or participators. Indulging in gossip, allows the one listening, watching or reading to suddenly set their problems aside whether similar or insimiliar and focus on others lives; all in which is wrong and hurtful. The best way to understand its inflicted wounds is to imagine that if that person being targeted was you!

Earthly riches can assist in temporary happiness, but also comes with the price of more responsibility. The most true long lasting happiness and peace is only found in our Heavenly Father.

The True Celebrity is God, our Creator. He defends and protects from the enemy, the weak and the strong, the rich and the poor, and the sick and the healthy. From His personal wallet does mankind's riches come, He provides the opportunity, wisdom and knowledge to attain the wealth received. It is not by the efforts of mankind, but the wisdom and strength given to push toward the efforts, to receive the success. Since Our Creator, is the Respecter of no particular person (s), the blessings provided for one, are attainable through asking in prayer, for all. He has promised in His word, that *"He has come for us to live life abundantly."*

Masking Our Happiness . . . .

Article By: Mia F. Stubbs

So many times I have masked my happiness, so that my friends and enemies would not assume weaknesses.

Talking with someone that I had just met at the library. I shared things in my life that were most uncomfortable for me. From the outside, like me, he appeared to have all T's crossed and I's dotted. Feeling impressed to share a few of my most deepest storms with him, such as gossip, how it had affected my life, and God's thoughts on gossip, He listened and then asked, do you mind if I share something with you, I listened to him, and after listening to him, he seemed so relieved. Sharing my experiences with him, minimum or maximum opened up a path of healing that he didn't even realize needed fixing.

Anger results from uncommunicated feelings. Speaking or writing about your feelings is therapeutic for the listener and reader, and is therapy for the giver!

Chapter 3

What Does God Say About "Gossip"

References from NIV and KJV Bible

~Leviticus 19:16
   "Thou shall not go up and down as a talebearer among thy people: neither shall thou stand against the blood of thy neighbor; I am the LORD. *(King James Version)*

~Psalm 15:3
   He that backbitten not with his tongue, nor doeth evil to his neighbor, nor taketh up a reproach against his neighbour. *(King James Version)*

~Psalm 41:6
   And if he come to see me, he speaketh vanity: his heart gathereth iniquity to itself; when he goeth abroad, he telleth it. *(King James Version)*

~Psalm 69:12
   They that sit in the gate speak against me; and I was the song of the drunkards. *(King James Version)*

~Proverbs 11:13
   A talebearer revealeth secrets: but he that is of a faithful spirit concealeth the matter. *(King James Version)*

~Proverbs 16:28
   A froward man soweth strife: and a whisperer separateth chief friends. *(King James Version)*

~Proverbs 17:4
   A wicked doer giveth heed to false lips; and a liar giveth ear to a naughty tongue. *(King James Version)*

~Proverbs 25:10
   Lest he that heareth it put thee to shame, and thine infamy turn not away. *(King James Version)*

*Others may accuse you of **gossip**, and you will never regain your good reputation. (New Living Translation)*

~Proverbs 25:23

The north wind driveth away rain: so doth an angry countenance a backbiting tongue. *(King James Version)*

*As surely as a north wind brings rain, so a **gossip**ing tongue causes anger! (New Living Translation)*

~Proverbs 26:20

Where no wood is, there the fire goeth out: so where there is no talebearer, the strife ceaseth. *(King James Version)*

*Fire goes out without wood, and quarrels disappear when **gossip** stops. (New Living Translation)*

~Romans 1:29

Being filled with all unrighteousness, fornication, wickedness, covetousness, maliciousness; full of envy, murder, debate, deceit, malignity; whisperers. *(King James Version)*

*Their lives became full of every kind of wickedness, sin, greed, hate, envy, murder, quarreling, deception, malicious behavior, and **gossip**. (New Living Translation)*

~2 Corinthians 12:20

For I fear, lest, when I come, I shall not find you such as I would, and that I shall be found unto you such as ye would not: lest there be debates, envyings, wraths, strifes, backbitings, whisperings, swellings, tumults. *(King James Version)*

*For I am afraid that when I come I won't like what I find, and you won't like my response. I am afraid that I will find quarreling, jealousy, anger, selfishness, slander, **gossip**, arrogance, and disorderly behavior. (New Living Translation)*

~1 Timothy 5:13

And withal they learn to be idle, wandering about from house to house; and not only idle, but tattlers also and busybodies, speaking things which they ought not. (King James Version)

*And if they are on the list, they will learn to be lazy and will spend their time **gossip**ing from house to house, meddling in other people's business and talking about things they shouldn't. (New Living Translation)*

What Does God Say About "Rumors"...

References from NIV and KJV Bible

~Exodus 23:1
Thou shalt not raise a false report: put not thine hand with the wicked to be an unrighteous witness. *(King James Version)*

*You must not pass along false **rumors**. You must not cooperate with evil people by lying on the witness stand. (New Living Translation)*

~Job 28:22
Destruction and death say, We have heard the fame thereof with our ears. *(King James Version)*

*Destruction [Hebrew Abaddon.] and Death say,' we've heard only **rumors** of where wisdom can be found.' (New Living Translation)*

~Psalm 31:13
For I have heard the slander of many: fear was on every side: while they took counsel together against me, they devised to take away my life. *(King James Version)*

*I have heard the many **rumors** about me, and I am surrounded by terror. My enemies conspire against me, plotting to take my life. (New Living Translation)*

~Proverbs 18:8
The words of a talebearer are as wounds, and they go down into the innermost parts of the belly. *(King James Version)*

~Proverbs 26:22

The words of a talebearer are as wounds, and they go down into the innermost parts of the belly. *(King James Version)*

Rumors *are dainty morsels that sink deep into one's heart. (New Living Translation)*

~Isaiah 23:1

The burden of Tyre. Howl, ye ships of Tarshish; for it is laid waste, so that there is no house, no entering in: from the land of Chittim it is revealed to them. *(King James Version)*

This message came to me concerning Tyre: Weep, O ships of Tarshish, for the harbor and houses of Tyre are gone! The **rumors** *you heard in Cyprus are all true. (New Living Translation)*

~Isaiah 58:9

Then shalt thou call, and the LORD shall answer; thou shalt cry, and he shall say, Here I am. If thou take away from the midst of thee the yoke, the putting forth of the finger, and speaking vanity. *(King James Version)*

Then when you call, the Lord will answer. 'Yes, I am here,' he will quickly reply. "Remove the heavy yoke of oppression. Stop pointing your finger and spreading vicious **rumors***! (New Living Translation)*

~Jeremiah 18:18

Then said they, Come and let us devise devices against Jeremiah; for the law shall not perish from the priest, nor counsel from the wise, nor the word from the prophet. Come, and let us smite him with the tongue, and let us not give heed to any of his words. *(King James Version)*

[A Plot against Jeremiah] Then the people said, "Come on, let's plot a way to stop Jeremiah. We have plenty of priests and wise men and prophets. We don't need him to teach the word and give us advice and prophecies. Let's spread **rumors** *about him and ignore what he says." (New Living Translation)*

~Jeremiah 20:10

For I heard the defaming of many, fear on every side. Report, say they, and we will report it. All my familiars watched for my halting, saying, Peradventure he will be enticed, and we shall prevail against him, and we shall take our revenge on him. (King James Version)

I have heard the many **rumors** about me. They call me "The Man Who Lives in Terror." They threaten, "If you say anything, we will report it." Even my old friends are watching me, waiting for a fatal slip. "He will trap himself," they say, "and then we will get our revenge on him." (New Living Translation)

~Jeremiah 51:46

And lest your heart faint, and ye fear for the rumour that shall be heard in the land; a rumour shall both come one year, and after that in another year shall come a rumour, and violence in the land, ruler against ruler. (King James Version)

But do not panic; don't be afraid when you hear the first rumor of approaching forces. For **rumors** will keep coming year by year. Violence will erupt in the land as the leaders fight against each other. (New Living Translation)

~Acts 21:24

Them take, and purify thyself with them, and be at charges with them, that they may shave their heads: and all may know that those things, whereof they were informed concerning thee, are nothing; but that thou thyself also walkest orderly, and keepest the law. (King James Version)

Go with them to the Temple and join them in the purification ceremony, paying for them to have their heads ritually shaved. Then everyone will know that the **rumors** are all false and that you yourself observe the Jewish laws. (New Living Translation)

What does God Says about Speaking Untruth: "Lies" . . .

References from NIV and KJV Bible

Psalm 26:4

I have not sat with vain persons, neither will I go in with dissemblers. (King James Version)

I do not spend time with **liars** or go along with hypocrites. (New Living Translation)

~Psalm 43:1
Judge me, O God, and plead my cause against an ungodly nation: O deliver me from the deceitful and unjust man. (King James Version)

Declare me innocent, O God! Defend me against these ungodly people. Rescue me from these unjust **liars**. (New Living Translation)

~Psalm 55:23
But thou, O God, shalt bring them down into the pit of destruction: bloody and deceitful men shall not live out half their days; but I will trust in thee. (King James Version)

But you, O God, will send the wicked down to the pit of destruction. Murderers and **liars** will die young, but I am trusting you to save me. (New Living Translation)

~Psalm 63:11
But the king shall rejoice in God; every one that sweareth by him shall glory: but the mouth of them that speak lies shall be stopped. (King James Version)

But the king will rejoice in God. All who trust in him will praise him, while **liars** will be silenced. (New Living Translation)

~Psalm 101:7
He that worketh deceit shall not dwell within my house: he that telleth lies shall not tarry in my sight. (King James Version)

I will not allow deceivers to serve in my house, and **liars** will not stay in my presence. (New Living Translation)

~Psalm 120:2

Deliver my soul, O LORD, from lying lips, and from a deceitful tongue. *(King James Version)*

*Rescue me, O Lord, from **liars** and from all deceitful people.* *(New Living Translation)*

~Proverbs 6:12

A naughty person, a wicked man, walketh with a froward mouth. *(King James Version)*

*What are worthless and wicked people like? They are constant **liars**.* *(New Living Translation)*

~Proverbs 17:4

A wicked doer giveth heed to false lips; and a liar giveth ear to a naughty tongue. *(King James Version)*

*Wrongdoers eagerly listen to gossip; **liars** pay close attention to slander.*

~Proverbs 29:12

If a ruler hearken to lies, all his servants are wicked. *(King James Version)*

*If a ruler pays attention to **liars**, all his advisers will be wicked.* *(New Living Translation)*

~Isaiah 57:4

Against whom do ye sport yourselves? against whom make ye a wide mouth, and draw out the tongue? are ye not children of transgression, a seed of falsehood. *(King James Version)*

*Whom do you mock, making faces and sticking out your tongues? You children of sinners and **liars**!* *(New Living Translation)*

~Jeremiah 9:2

Oh that I had in the wilderness a lodging place of wayfaring men; that I might leave my people, and go from them! for they be all adulterers, an assembly of treacherous men. (King James Version)

Oh, that I could go away and forget my people and live in a travelers' shack in the desert. For they are all adulterers—a pack of treacherous **liars**. (New Living Translation)

~Hosea 7:1

When I would have healed Israel, then the iniquity of Ephraim was discovered, and the wickedness of Samaria: for they commit falsehood; and the thief cometh in, and the troop of robbers spoileth without. (King James Version)

I want to heal Israel, [Hebrew Ephraim, referring to the northern kingdom of Israel; also in 7:8, 11.] but its sins are too great. Samaria is filled with **liars**. Thieves are on the inside and bandits on the outside! (New Living Translation)

~Malachi 3:5

And I will come near to you to judgment; and I will be a swift witness against the sorcerers, and against the adulterers, and against false swearers, and against those that oppress the hireling in his wages, the widow, and the fatherless, and that turn aside the stranger from his right, and fear not me, saith the LORD of hosts. (King James Version)

"At that time I will put you on trial. I am eager to witness against all sorcerers and adulterers and **liars**. I will speak against those who cheat employees of their wages, who oppress widows and orphans, or who deprive the foreigners living among you of justice, for these people do not fear me," says the Lord of Heaven's Armies. (New Living Translation)

~Revelation 2:2

I know thy works, and thy labour, and thy patience, and how thou canst not bear them which are evil: and thou hast tried them which say they are apostles, and are not, and hast found them liars. (King James Version)

*I know all the things you do. I have seen your hard work and your patient endurance. I know you don't tolerate evil people. You have examined the claims of those who say they are apostles but are not. You have discovered they are **liars**. (New Living Translation)*

~Revelation 3:9

Behold, I will make them of the synagogue of Satan, which say they are Jews, and are not, but do lie; behold, I will make them to come and worship before thy feet, and to know that I have loved thee. *(King James Version)*

*Look, I will force those who belong to Satan's synagogue—those **liars** who say they are Jews but are not—to come and bow down at your feet. They will acknowledge that you are the ones I love. (New Living Translation)*

~Revelation 21:8

But the fearful, and unbelieving, and the abominable, and murderers, and whoremongers, and sorcerers, and idolaters, and all liars, shall have their part in the lake which burneth with fire and brimstone: which is the second death. *(King James Version)*

*But cowards, unbelievers, the corrupt, murderers, the immoral, those who practice witchcraft, idol worshipers, and all **liars**—their fate is in the fiery lake of burning sulfur. This is the second death." (New Living Translation)*

Chapter 4

THE EFFECTS OF GOSSIP . . .

The affects of gossip has been discussed several times in this book. Gossip of the tongue is lethal, and the effects it leaves on its targets are deadly. The enemy has used several methods of attempting to destroy mankind; gossip of the mind, is his most devious tool. If he can control the way all of mankind thinks, or better yet manipulate a thought in the mind, through false insinuations, this could be the masterpiece in destroying mankind. To add the icing on the cake, for the best indirect dart, why not use mankind to be the tools he used to create gossip among one another. This clever, crafty evil and hateful enemy thought if he can have mankind destroy one another, through his subtle indirect approach, surely he would have the chance he has always wanted, of ruling the world.

The enemy started his first approach in Heaven when God allowed him to take one third of the angels and was removed from Heaven before the presence of God. That was not enough for the enemy, he then slipped an indirect approach when he spoke through the serpent, and deceived Eve into temptation and disobeying God; and many of God's children, mankind thereafter. God always wants His creations to be victorious over the enemy, and our minds to be sharp. He says for us to be *"Wise as a serpent, harmless as a dove"* God wants us to be winners in Him.

But we must start by exposing how the enemy has used gossip of the mind to be the cause of so many sicknesses. If we are sick, how can we be strong enough to win the battles! So the enemy desires and attempts to enslave mankind, keep them confused, hurt, depressed, suicidal, for then, their God given gifts have been disabled due to their distraction.

There are so many types of depression inflicted due to gossip by the enemy, I would like to share just a few:

*   **Depressed Moods**—A feeling of deep sadness and that you are helpless to deal with your life and that the situation is hopeless. These depressive symptoms can feel overwhelming.

- **Anhedonia**—The loss of interest and pleasure from things you used to enjoy. Loss of life and sense of joy. This depression symptom along with depressed moods, are strong indicators of depression.
- **Irritability**—Even the little things can bother you and you are easily annoyed. Your tolerance levels are low and you may feel irritable, agitated or restless.
- **Low Self-Esteem**—Those experiencing depression often feel worthless and may also have feelings of guilt. These negative views are persistent and we can lose faith and hope for the future.
- **Sleep Disturbances**—Either sleeping too much or difficulty sleeping can be depression symptoms. It is not unusual for those suffering from depression to wake up during the night or too early and be unable to get back to sleep. Another depressive symptom would be sleeping much more than you normally would.
- **Changes in Weight**—Those seeking relief from depression may eat too much or due to Anhedonia may lose interest in eating and lose their appetite resulting in sometimes dramatic weight changes.
- **Fatigue and Low Energy**—Feeling tired and not having any energy are common depression symptoms. Even after waking in the morning you may feel as tired as if you hadn't slept at all. Everything seems to take an extra effort and even body movements can be slow including speech that may become slow and spoken in a monotone.
- **Poor Concentration and Impaired Thinking**—Depression causes some to lose their mental focus. Concentration is lost and clear thinking becomes more difficult. Memory is also affected.

Other ways are through the use of drugs, alcoholism, serious health conditions. It breaks God's heart to see His children feeling such pain and rejection. It is not His will for His inherited children to go through this, for this was the whole purpose of sending His Son; that through His death all things have been conquered.

"Gossip and it's deadly affects are compared to, a person sleeping peacefully and soundly, then suddenly they are attacked by an intruder. Not expecting this attack, they are startled, and cannot fight back due to being in a sleep stupor"

"Gossip is also considered murder or rape of the tongue. Is the gossiper any better than a murderer or rapist in God's Eyes?"

People are not born hurt, but born as babies, perfect. Life experiences hit, some harder than others to the weak and the strong. Some recover quickly and others it takes a little bit more time and support. Aren't our jobs as creations by God to work in harmony with one another?

People that are guilty of gossiping, but willing to make a change before God, receive what is stated in truth about gossip and it's affects to others, and genuinely will change. But others guilty of gossip and do not want to change before God, become every critical of why gossips disease is being made a issue, due to their own guilt. This also hurts God!

Personally feeling the effects of gossip, and knowing that many lives have been destroyed due to the affects of gossip, saddens my heart. Shame on any part takers in ruining ones character, though you might not fear man, you should fear God, and know that He is watching, waiting, listening and very protective of His children. And since He too was affected by gossip by the enemy, this is something He looks into personally. For our cares, are His cares!

God is waiting for you; will you do this for Him? And most of all, will you do it for that person that is really in need of a positive word, or in need of someone to stand up or speak up for them?

God Uses Rumors . . .

Article by: Mia F. Stubbs

The Angels of God was sent to Mary the Virgin, to tell her that she would be impregnated with the Holy Spirit, and that she would call His Name, Jesus, for He would be our Savior through dying for our sins.

In all the excitement, Mary the Virgin and soon to be Mother of Jesus, did not realize the implications that would be connected to her powerful news of becoming a mother of "A King!"

Picture the people in her village, spreading rumors and gossiping about matters that they did not understand. You can picture them saying, "She's not a Virgin, she has been with Joseph before marriage to him" though she never responded to their hurtful accusations, I am sure that those words spoken, really hurt~

God shared a special message with Mary the Virgin and Joseph that He did not share with those in the village. God can use anything, even rumors, what He shares with one person; He does not always share with another. We must not let man dictate what our circumstances appear, from their eyes.

What has God promised you in your circumstances that He has not shared with anyone else? If from their eyes, the one's that are judging or gossiping; it seems God has abandoned you, do not worry! For they are looking from the Non-Eye of God, just remember what God has told you in your spirit, which is connected to His Spirit! Man only sees up the street, but God, whom not only sees around the corner, has designed the whole block!

Our Enemies Are Our Footstool . . .

Article by: Mia F. Stubbs

Read Romans 12:14

"Bless those who persecute you; bless and do not curse"

In life when you are wronged by someone, God says your reward is in Heaven, but you also receive a taste of it on earth.

Our favor that we receive in life, which is circumstantial, according to the blessing promised by our Father, is payment from God, for going through something for His Namesake. God has promised when we go through something for Him, He owes us and He pays all His debts on time.

If our enemies only knew, each time, that they had been influenced to hurt us, that they actually set us up in a position to receive a huge blessing, that we were not suppose to receive, they would always be kind to us!

Thank God for friends and enemies and all the contributions they make in our lives!

Prayer: Dear God help us to love our enemies as well as our friends, so that then You are glorified!

Thought of the day: It takes more energy to carry the hurt, then it does when the hurt is released.

Chapter 5

RECOGNIZING YOUR GOSSIPING . . .

Psalms 41:6 "And if he come to see me, he speaketh vanity: his heart gathereth iniquity to itself; when he goeth abroad, he telleth it."

It is not hard recognizing when you're gossiping. Ask yourself these three questions to determine if you are a participant of gossip:

1. If God was standing right next to me, would He approve of this conversation?

2. Is the person I am discussing, present, to defend themselves?

3. If the tables were turned, would I like this to be said about me or one of my loved ones?

If the answers above were each answered "*yes*," then there have not been any errors of one's character being destroyed.

Outside of asking if God would approve of the conversation; is this conversation something that you need to ask a person that you care about? And should it be asked in private? In no way should anyone be placed in a position to be embarrassed and made to feel that their private details true or false are the root of conversation, for entertainment and amusement for the group for that day, or any other day!

Individuals that gossip can be cured of their disease, very quickly! And this is by; placing the shoe from the foot of the person (s) being attacked with the rumors, and placing it directly on your own foot.

God is asking you to stop gossiping, will you do this for Him? He really loves you, and He really loves the person (s) in who are being gossiped about.

Gossip & Recovery . . .

Article by: Mia F. Stubbs

In a lawsuit, you're suing for pain and suffering, the emotional and physical drain . . .

In a case where the plaintiff has been hurt in an accident, their life has been abruptly torn apart in that split second by an irresponsible driver.

Yes they might eventually be healed and recover, but will they ever be the same as they once were before they afflicted with this pain?

Most unfortunate when the irresponsible driver that has caused this disturbance in this victim's life, is given a smack on the hand, and are able to move on with their life, while yet the victim has to redirection their life according to their unwarranted added circumstance.

This is another example of how gossip is penetrated on its victim. The gossiper has spread the rumors, the damage is done, and now the victim's inner happiness has been robbed, not only is there one victim, but the family becomes a victim, the ones that have always been so close to them have also been robbed of that once 100% of their hurt loved-one's attention; though that bond between them can never be broken, life has left a temporary disturbance.

But God who is watching and listening uses these once afflicted souls for His Glory and pays His children that had to endure such discomfort a long term severance payment of favor for their pain and suffering.

Chapter 6

THE TRUE IMPORTANCE OF SAYING NO

WEAPON FORMED . . .

In God's Word . . .

Isaiah 54:17 "No weapon that is formed against thee shall prosper; and every tongue that shall rise against thee in judgment thou shalt condemn. This is the heritage of the servants of the LORD, and their righteousness is of me, saith the LORD." (King James Version)

Interpretation: "No weapon that has been made to be used against you will succeed. You will have an answer for anyone who accuses you. This is the inheritance of the LORD's servants. Their victory comes from me," declares the LORD." (God's Word Interpretation)

Bible in Basic English: "No instrument of war which is formed against you will be of any use; and every tongue which says evil against you will be judged false. This is the heritage of the servants of the Lord, and their righteousness comes from me, says the Lord."

The true purpose of "No weapon formed shall prosper" is to protect the mind of the person being targeted by the enemy, whether it is the enemy gossiping, manipulating, using false insinuations to the mind, or the enemy using an individual while in casual conversation to tear down the spirit of another. The main tool as stated previously in this book is that the enemy uses gossip to destroy the mind of mankind. The enemy loves to try to bully God's beautiful children, and the main way is through gossip of the mind.

From the beginning of time, the enemy has tried to use gossip of the mind, manipulation and insinuations of the mind to removed God's children off the path designed by God. This fact is evident when he cunningly convinced one third of the angels to turn against God in Heaven. It was even more evident when he deceived and convinced Eve that disobedience to God would be more profitable to her, then obedience to God.

The powerful phrase, "No weapon formed against you, shall prosper," has been given as the answer key for mankind to walk in victory physically, spiritually and mentally. This powerful phrase is designed to be the cushioned pillow of peace, to sleep at night. It is the mental medicine of the mind, body and soul.

The enemy has unfortunately tried to convince mankind that there is no power in speaking with authority God's words for us, "No weapon formed against you shall prosper." The tactic he used, was to have mankind feel as though such powerful words stated in the Bible, given by God, Our Creator, were made simply for those in the Bible at that time, and that any passage stated in God's word, holds no weight of power now. This is another deception of the enemy, to try to handicap God's children, so that we will feel that there is no hope. This is his way of being a bully to the mind. This is the very reason why God created this verse, so that we would have a weapon to fight back against the enemy, to protect our mind.

How many times in conversation, have you been sharing with someone something great in life you would like to do? Some healing you would like to receive; and somewhere in the conversation, the enemy has used that person to tell you that your desired plans will not work, or your healing may not come, or will not come. Recognize that is the spirit of the enemy using that individual without them even knowing it. God has promised in His word, that He has already conquered the world, and all that we need to be victorious, through His blood. So all things are attainable in Him, wisdom, knowledge, healing, our desires, whatever we seek to allow us to progress forward, has already been conquered through Him.

God in His infinite wisdom, created Adam and Eve, with His powerful breath. He formed their bodies with the dust of the earth, and He breathed His breath of life in them, supplying them, our first earthly parents with the power to speak wealth over themselves with just, their mere words. The powerful luxury of speaking powerful words of wealth was included with the benefits in His selfless creation of mankind. Our Father's breathe is the life line of all mankind today. The powerful luxury given by Our

Heavenly Father as a gift to our first earthly parents is the same powerful gift all of mankind possesses today.

This powerful gift of divine breathe, given from Our Creator, allows us to speak the wealth of physical, mental, spiritual, and financial into our personal life. And the powerful phrase, given as the answer key in the bible, "No weapon formed against us shall prosper," protects us from the enemy trying to rob us mentally of the gifts of wealth we seek physically, mentally, spiritually, and financially. The enemy believes and fears God's power, and also fears mankind possessing full understanding in utilizing these gifts given by God.

Our Heavenly Creator created our first earthly parents, Adam and Eve in His own Image, after His likeness and gave them dominion over all the earth. Adam was even given the privileged by Our Creator, of naming every earthly creature created. Such privileges given to earth's first created man produced even more envy and rage in the enemy. Jealousy of God's power and now rage toward God's creation of mankind. This also became the ground rules of the enemy wanting to try to destroy all of God's creation. Though our Creator had the enemy removed from Heaven and cast on earth, because of the enemy's evil tactics after Our Father pleading for him to change, all rights he had been given to claim, were immediately diminished. Dominion over the earth has been given to mankind.

In creating our first earthly parents, Adam and Eve; our Heavenly Father created them with such a powerful mind full of wisdom, knowledge, spiritual gifts and the spirit of discernment against the evil forces of the enemy. Our earthly first parent's mental capacity was used at 100%. Allowing them and their seed birthed through them, a very strong capacity to remember every detail told to them centuries before. Imagine our first earthly parent and the seed birthed through them, would not lack any form of memory lost, as long as they were to remain obedient to God and not fall into the temptations conjured by the enemy.

Unfortunately, the enemy knew and understood this concept. The enemy, through deception and gossip of the mind, manipulated mankind to sin. The enemy knew if sin was brought upon the earth it would result in mankind's mental capacity decreasing. As a result, our first earthly parents and their seed after them were decreased in height and mental capacity.

The mental capacity being reduced because of sin in the earth was all a part of the enemies plan. God knowing this, gave us the opportunity He did not provide for the enemy; He sent His Son to mankind, as our Savior and earthly Example to redeem all destruction; the satanic plans of the enemy. In the first chapter of John, *"In the beginning was the Word, and the Word was with God, and the Word was God."*

Our Infinite Creator, knowing the beginning from the end, knew that due to Him giving His ultimate creation, mankind, the choice of being a free moral agent, having freedom of choice; that if sin was committed through disobedience in Him, that sin would decrease the earth and most of all mankind. This once powerfully strong mental capacity given for mankind would be weakened; resulting into complete disaster and the earth being completely ruled by the enemy. So Our Wonderful Creator sent His only begotten Son, Jesus to redeem the world, mankind. His Son's, blood made all things new, it conquered every sin that could ever be committed by mankind, it redeemed mankind of the powerful spiritual gifts once tampered with by the enemy.

The bible was written as a guide for mankind, a comfort to our soul, how to live a victorious life and a constant reminder of God's powerful ability in conquering any circumstance. It was also written to assist man as a daily reminder of His laws of the earth. As stated previously, due to sin; mankind's memory decreased from remembering things told to them centuries before. Our Heavenly Father always wanting to enable us, instead of disabling, gave us His Son in human flesh and the bible as a text flesh tool to read daily, a consistent mental reminder of Him.

The enemy on the other hand, tries to blind mankind with his tactic of gossip of the mind through manipulation, and insinuation, to not believe in the laws of the bible; not to believe the power of wealth in each page. This evil being's tactic is to confuse and blind mankind, of our true God given rights. This jealous and very hateful perpetrator of mankind wants to disable, handicap us, to enslave us mentally. But he can't because God has given these gifts, and a great awakening is being received by many of mankind; (Amen).

Hearing the verse as a child, and even as an adult; I never really gave thought to its power, till I was faced with a particular situation. A good example of the importance of reading, understanding and speaking these powerful words "No weapon formed" was when talking to someone about writing this book. Talking with a co worker at work, in which I respected his opinions about various things, I decided to share an article I had written concerning gossip and how it had affected my life. Upon giving him the paper with the article that I wrote he immediately began to ask repeatedly why was I writing this. At that time, in the article that I had written, I did not include a bible text in the article that would back up the basis of how gossip was a sin, and most of all how it had affected me and many others. This person I respected highly began telling me that the article was without reason and point, and even pointed out to me, that I did not show any proof in my writings, bible texts, to prove that gossip is a sin.

Though a follower of God, my dear friend, in whom I respected and many times listen to for such encouraging words, did not understand for that moment that another spirit had overtaken him. Though I did not realize it at first, that a ungodly spirit used him to discourage me from expressing a powerful issue that has and is affecting so many others including myself today; I became very discouraged, and began to even wonder if the painful results gossip, once used by the enemy to break my spirit was even worth speaking out about, through expression of my writings. I began to question whether God really wanted me to write of my expressions, and most of all, was it truly a sin? God spoke to me in my spirit, and told me to keep moving forward. In His word it states in *2 Timothy 1:7 "For God hath not given us the spirit of fear; but of power, and of love, and of a sound mind."* God reminded me of His word that states in *Isaiah 54:17 "No weapon that is formed against thee shall prosper; and every tongue that shall rise against thee in judgment thou shalt condemn. This is the heritage of the servants of the LORD, and their righteousness is of me, saith the LORD."*

Because he was someone that I respected as a follower of God, I felt that God must have been speaking through him, that I should just keep quiet, and one day my pain of gossip would drift away. Weeks later, that same friend came to me and apologized that he said such things to me, and that what I had wrote, in expression of my hurt was right, and to stay on my path.

Though I have read and heard this powerful verse before, I never gave thought to just how powerful this verse among many was. I began reading it over and over again, picturing God saying this verse to me with great power! I became so excited that I shared this powerful verse with my son. I began explaining to him, if he is ever in conversation with anyone, child or adult, and if he feels that the conversation is bringing him discouragement and not encouragement in his spirit, to very kindly, right away say, "No Weapon Formed!" This will right away, shun away the spirit that had overtaken that individual for that quick moment.

If I had of right away responded to my friend kindly, by saying, I am sorry you do not understand at this point, but God will explain it to you at the right time, "No Weapon Formed!" This bold and powerful statement would have cut the conversation short, and I would have walked away, burden free, it would have given me power over the spirit that for that moment had taken over him to discourage my spirit. But since I sat and listen to what he said, even though I knew in my spirit that this is what God wanted me to do, I began having the temporary feelings for days of wanting to give up.

Another example is; I have always wanted to be in business, even as a child. I was sharing with someone how I had ventured in another new business; I was so excited while sharing it with them. When I shared with them the name of the business, she right away began telling me that a friend of hers had joined this business, but was not successful, and that it might not work for me. I very kindly responded to her by saying with a smile, *"No Weapon Formed, Shall Prosper . . . Greater is He in me, than He that is in the world! . . . My blessing might not be hers, and hers might not be mine . . ."* After walking away from her, I felt such a peace. The spirit that had overtaken her for that moment and then attempted to use her to discourage my thinking had now been shunned with my authority in speaking such words of power. *"No Weapon Formed Shall Prosper."*

If I had of sat and listened to what she was telling me concerning the business long enough, and had not spoke with authority from God's word to shoot down the invisible darts aimed toward my mental thinking, concerning the business venture, I would have given the enemy power over my blessing. My lack of belief, mixed with her lack of belief would have produced no progress.

God has given to mankind in His word, powerful verses for us to use as a sword to slice the attacks of the enemy. The enemy has manipulated gossip to the mind through insinuation and manipulation, to God's children, mankind so much that they are made to feel these verses do not apply to their life's circumstance. Powerful texts given by God for our victory in life has been made so watered down to the point, where many have forgotten the true meaning.

For example, you are in a restaurant, and someone sneezes, the first thing anyone would say, is "God Bless You," that powerful statement said, has just blessed that person's life, it has protected them from harm, and has opened a path where they might not have even known they needed it from our Creator. God, Our Creator, knowing that this person needed this blessing, allowed them to sneeze so they could be blessed through someone, by Him; in whatever area they are in need of being blessed by Him. God is a Spirit, He uses of His creation to accomplish His various tasks. He in return puts the power behind it to make the task complete. God does not need mankind to do any works for Him; only through Him can the works be completed. The point of our Loving Creator Co-Operating with His Creation is so that everything is worked according to His planned operation.

The same way "God Bless You" has been watered down, so has *"No Weapon Formed Shall Prosper . . ." Greater Is He That Is In Me, Than He That Is In The World."* In this same way the enemy has tried to gossip to the mind that these powerful phrases were only good in the days of those in the bible, but hold no weight today. This is a deception. Men and women created in the beginning had no need for books to read, for every detailed instruction given by God to mankind was able to be remembered for centuries later. Our Creator of unconditional love had the bible wrote as a testament of His Son and His power. He also did not want His children to be bullied by the enemy. So He provided a means of a shielded armor to protect us from the tactics of the enemy, for when he attempts to use gossip of the mind through insinuations and manipulations. Our loving Creator would never leave His children without tools and great access through His word to receive His power of assistance.

If ever in conversation with someone, and the conversation suddenly becomes a subtracter of your spirit, instead of an adder to your spirit, with power, like you mean it, please right away, shun the enemy by saying, "No Weapon Formed Against Me Shall Prosper!" You will experience the peace in victory that God has designed for you to receive.

Words, Trailed By Only God's Power . . .

Article By: Mia F. Stubbs

Are our words powerful when we speak? Before God created the earth, He thoroughly thought of all His creations. He could have thought all things into existence, without speaking, due to His great power. But instead He spoke with His powerful words, all creations into existence. Most wonder why God, Our Heavenly Father of Greatness and Power, spoke creation into existence rather than just thinking it into existence alone.

I imagine that Our Heavenly Father thought, planned and then spoke all His creation into existence, for the purpose of an example for us. Just as He sent an Example through His Precious Son, Jesus; Whom came to earth to save us from our sins. When creating Adam and Eve, He formed our original earthly mother and father bodies, from the dust of the ground, following with breathing His breath of life into them.

Every breath that we breathe is borrowed from Our Master Supplier, Our Father, Whom allows us to tap into a portion of His Great Power through our positive thinking and speaking! Our thoughts and then spoken words of victory are so powerful that at even at our weakest point, because His breathe is in us, we actually are very strong!

Though this is very exciting, for those thinking what if someone uses their powerful gift of words against their enemies, for harm. Well, we can be of great courage! We are cursed daily by the enemy, whom uses our enemies to curse us through false predictions, words of hurt, gossip and any other hurtful way. But God Whom is over all, Whom is All-Powerful, watches over His children and all words that are spoken against us, He sends His Power with the words spoken that are aimed for our victory in all of our circumstances!

God has given us several darts to aim toward satan, whom in return, uses our enemies. God's word says, to say, "No weapon formed against you shall prosper!" These words are so powerful, when said; it right away shuns the enemy, from playing a mind game with us. The enemy knows his words aren't powerful, only Our Heavenly Father. So he will try to attack us through storing in our mind, the thoughts that are spoken against

77

us. It is like playing the game, "Space Invaders", you aim and shoot the bombs before they come anywhere near you. When you say, "No weapon formed," it shoots the enemy before he has a chance to store the mental game thought. I am so thankful God has conquered all of victory for us, and have also given us power through our words to do so!

God Co-Operates through giving us tools. In need of victory! Think positive, and then speak out the words of victory, and watch God send His power, to complete the transaction!

Chapter 7

GOSSIP AND HOW IT AFFECT MY LIFE . . .

Sharing Of Knowledge . . .

Articles By: Mia F. Stubbs

Sharing of knowledge of spoken or written experiences produces healing for the one speaking and writing, and prevention of mistakes to the one listening or reading!

Our experiences make us a winner, when shared with others!

Though I understand that I am not alone in facing gossip, I feel that it is imperative for my inner healing, to share how it personally affected my life. Being one of the targets of gossip in the past, was a tool the enemy used, to try and stop the processed plan God has destined for me. It was not visible to me, in the very beginning. In explanation, I did not recognize in the beginning, that the enemy was using the gossip to deter me off the path that God had set up for me. I honestly believe now, that people that passed rumors against me and others, did not realize that behind the curtains, the enemy was the real gossip manipulator. Those that have inflicted hurt, I am sure at times, did not know that the enemy was using them, just as a puppet on strings.

This book is to open the eyes of those that have not been aware on the most important tactics of the enemy, Gossip! From my personal experience and seeing how many people do not pay close attention to subtleness of the enemy, but are more attentive to the visible, evident ploys of this cunning creature. The enemy has from the beginning of time, used Gossip to affect individual lives in the church, the schools, the workplace, marriages, and our communities.

The main purpose of writing the book about "Gossip" was to exploit the enemy from behind the curtains. The enemy used gossip, something most would think of as a minor problem, to detour God's children and those to come, off their path! Many do not think of gossip as huge problem, but this is all a ploy by the enemy to minimize sin, and cause man to fall. Now that many are made aware of how gossip does affect many lives, and where gossip has actually stemmed from, many will want to be alert of it, for the betterment of increasing the family of Christ.

I feel compelled that it is not only essential in my healing process, but therapeutic to those that have ever been made to feel the stresses of gossip, as I once did, to share my experience of gossip. Speaking out about your experiences can be a great comfort or prevention of hurt for many others. In reference to myself, in no way, do I want to present myself as a woman without flaws, or a perfect follower of God and I am not quick in any way to call myself a Christian without sin and mistakes. "Christian" means Christ like in thoughts, actions and speaking. Some of these things I am still yet working toward. I am however, a woman finding my way through God, to His kingdom, aiming toward being a better Christian, and am woman enough to admit my faults. Trying daily to become a better example for my child; in who will outshine all my endeavors and accomplishments, without pain and sorrow. It is my true hope to one day, hear God say, *"Well done my good and faithful servants."*

The definition of a *"Christian:"*

- Professing belief in Jesus as Christ or following the religion based on the life and teachings of Jesus.
- Relating to or derived from Jesus or Jesus' teachings.
- Manifesting the qualities or spirit of Jesus; Christ like.
- Relating to or characteristic of Christianity or its adherents.
- Showing a loving concern for others; humane.
- One who professes belief in Jesus as Christ or follows the religion based on the life and teachings of Jesus.
- One who lives according to the teachings of Jesus.

"Christian" which the true meaning is "Christ-like images of God", is a very serious and respected name that is a lot of time watered down. Resulting in, missing the many hurting souls coming to Christ, due to not seeing those persons through the Eyes of God. It is I am sure the goal for every soul that claims this position of being a Christian, to become a better Christian, this also includes: *sinless thoughts*, a *sinless mouth* and *sinless actions*. Jesus, born in human flesh, perfect, tempted just as mankind, but never sinned in anyway, is our only perfect Example of how to be a Christian.

Jesus our perfect Example on earth and now in Heaven, **did not gossip,** but **was gossiped about** by His own. The enemy used the Pharisees and Sadducees, to destroy the character of Jesus, and attempted to make a mockery of Who He really was, the Son of God. *1 Timothy 3:16, "And without controversy great is the mystery of godliness: God was manifest in the flesh, justified in the Spirit, seen of angels, preached unto the Gentiles, believed on in the world, received up into glory."*

The bible speaks of, *Matthew 25:40, "And the King shall answer and say unto them, Verily I say unto you, Inasmuch as ye have done it unto one of the least of these my brethren, ye have done it unto me."* If those that are followers of God, called to be in the likeness of Christ, "Christians" are participating in gossip, the spread of rumors amongst their brethren, how much more different are they, then the Pharisees and Sadducees that made it their life endeavor to attempt to ridicule Jesus character and His true origin. Though they attempted, their efforts were not successful.

Bluntly speaking, if those that say they are in the likeness of Christ, what does this exemplify? Point the finger of their brethren sins, downsizing their own sin compared to their brethren sins, are not showing the likeness of Christ. One example being, participating in gossip, spreading rumors and/or any other sin, they may feel is small in God's Eyes. These sins in no way show the likeness of Christ, but are being used to be in the likeness of the true perpetrator, discussed in the beginning of this book. The bible states in James 2:10, *"For whosoever shall keep the whole law, and yet offend in one point, he is guilty of all."(KJV)* Translated for more clear understanding, *"If someone obeys all of God's laws except one, that person is guilty of breaking all of them."*

The enemy loves to make followers of God, feel as if their sins are small compared to others. It is a setup of thinking one is better than the next. But sin is sin; no sin is greater or lesser in the Eyes of God. We need not to be blinded by the enemy and make a note that we literally are no better than the next brethren, especially if participating in gossip;

spreading of rumors. God says in His word of *Ephesians 5:27 "That he might present it to himself a glorious church, not having spot, or wrinkle, or any such thing; but that it should be holy and without blemish."*

In creating earth and the fullness in the earth, Our Creator, created everything to grow upward to glorify Him. For example even the grass, flowers and trees grow upward to glorify Our Heavenly Father. Even when they nailed our Precious Jesus to the cross, the cross was raised upward. The purpose, though He was crucified without a cause, was to show His action of love, glorified God. There is no creation that God has made that had decreased in size, until the sin of mankind. As a result of sin, mankind tall framed stature, decreased in size. The longevity of man decreased. Because of sin, mankind would not live forever. The beauty of nature decreased. This is all in account to the enemy using gossip of the mind to deceive our first earthly parents, Adam and Eve.

The enemy's task at hand was to decrease the beauty of nature and mankind, but also to decrease the natural joy in serving God, through making many feel as if, when they become a Christian, their life would not change for better, but for the worst. Their life would not be full of increase but would only decrease. The enemy wanted many to believe that their trials and tribulations would not result in victory and happiness in Jesus. I can relate, for this is how the enemy wanted me to feel! God is restoring me with thoughts of joy!

My Life . . .

The knowledge that I have gained was taught through my personal experiences in my Heavenly Father. The past feelings of gossip and rejection have become my education and force in writing this book. And while I am still yet learning through His teachings, I would like to share what He has taught and is teaching me along the way!

I grew up in a very strict Christian home. My mother and father both, active in the church, and faithful tithe and stewardship stewards of God, set this as an example for my sisters and me. Though my parents thought it best to separate from their marriage while I was yet very young, my mother did her part as a mother and steward of God, to raise my sisters and I, in a strict and religious home.

Growing up, my sisters and I was never exposed to the secular things of the world, such as: watching any movies with a vulgar language and inappropriate behavior, attending any neighborhood or worldly parties, going to movie theaters, bowling alleys, amusement parks, unless these activities were planned by the church. We attended Christian schooling. We never ate meat, chicken, and were not allowed to have sugar, like candy or heavy sugared sweets. My mother prepared everything for us for the basis of good health and strong minds.

As children, my sisters and I thought it to be so embarrassing to be vegetarians. A lot our friends, that had grown up just as us, parents allowed them to eat meat and have some sugar. Of course my sisters and I felt we were really missing out on a lot. I remember, my mother would take us to Burger King for a whopper, no meat sandwich. At that time, Burger King's technology, was when you place your order, the person that would be ringing your order up, would have to repeat the order for the cook that was preparing the food, by saying, "We need four whoppers no meat with cheese, must be made fresh!" How hilarious! It seemed as if the person ringing up our order spoke in the microphone louder with our order than anyone else's order.

What is so profound, such things I found so embarrassing in my younger years, is the very basis of how many are utilizing, to live a healthier and fuller life today.

In my teen years, I attended a private Christian boarding high school, where I started feeling the beginning affects of gossip. I now realize that this gossip only stemmed from jealousies. My sisters had all attended boarding school, and I begged my mother to please allow me, being the youngest to go to boarding school. I attended boarding school in the 10th grade. I was so excited, thinking now I have some freedom. I had my first relationship in boarding school. I met him on the first day of orientation. Him being very outspoken, handsome and very popular, became my boyfriend. What I liked about him most, is that he never allowed people to dictate what he should do, or in whom he should date. He was very strong in character, which made me admire him.

A couple months after being at school, it was college days at boarding school for the weekend. This event was for alumni's that had previously attended, to visit the school. While the college guys were there, I met a guy, whom told me that there was going to be party off campus, and that me and a couple of the other ladies were invited. This guy told me that we would have to sneak out the dorm to go to the party. I must say, growing up in such a strict home, I was very naïve to a lot of things. I should have followed my inner spirit, and said, "No thanks . . . But never attending a party, it sounded like a lot of fun. I invited a few of the girls I knew, and told them we were invited to a party; they were just as excited as me. We left campus, and was unfortunately caught by the dean. I was suspended from school, and was very afraid of what my mother was going to do to me. Most of all I knew that my new boyfriend would be flooded with people giving him every reason why he should not be with me for sneaking off campus.

Upon returning back to school, gossip and rumors were at a larger scale. Anything that could be said against my character was said. My boyfriend at the time, understood me more than they did, after a while he overlooked and even defended me against such ridicule that was being said against my character. Through lots of resistance from a lot of the other ladies, we dated from 10th till graduation. I stood my ground, without fighting and arguments from those that did not care for me. I never had a feeling of fear, and did not allow anyone to push me into to doing anything I did not want to do, but I must say there was an uneasy feeling among my peers. I was very good at hiding my feelings; no one would know that they offended me through their actions of gossip.

It was the tradition that when you graduated from this boarding school, that you then attended its sister college, which was also a Christian college. Of course I did not want to attend, due to my name being demolished. The thought of going through such ridicule, and gossip with the same people again, was not something I wanted to experience. How I was treated at school through gossip only enhanced my desire of rebellion. At graduation day, my boyfriend and I decided together that a long term relationship would not work, and terminated our relationship.

And of course the gossipers, that had surrounded me at school, had relatives that had friends in my hometown church. The enemy used these rumors as a means of fashioning my rebellion. At church in my hometown, some of the members of course looked at me differently, only due to them seeing me through the eyes of those that had gossiped against me. I had in no way, any desire to go to church, so much said, why placed myself in this position for even just one day per week; though it was nothing compared to boarding school, yet!

Being older and wiser now, I realize that enemy used my feelings of experiencing the pains of gossip from my peers and others, also the feelings of being deprived as a tool to push me toward wanting to participate in secular activities, the desire for a change. With the feeling of my true character not being understood; I left home at age 18 years, with of course, no knowledge and experience of the world. I moved into an apartment with a friend. I began going out to clubs, and having what I thought at the time was good fun. I loved the attention I received. The excitement of it all is what drove me to want to go out to clubs more. I met new friends, and actually felt that my life was complete, no gossip, prejudgment.

I can only thank God now that He protected me from so many dangers that could have happen. Though I drank and experimented with smoking cigarettes, God allowed me to have a strong enough mind, to never get with the wrong crowd that would get me hooked on drugs or even becoming an alcoholic. Though I liked to go out to clubs and experience such excitement; there was a small part of me that felt very empty. I was experiencing the feeling of freedom that I had always wanted due to my strict upbringing, but there was still a part of me, that was missing something, not realizing that it was God. Once you are God's, He never lets you go. He is the perfect Gentleman; He patiently waits until you return back to Him.

I dated and was married at 20 years old. At age 21, I was pregnant with my beautiful son. My son has always been, outside of God, the joy of my life. During my pregnancy, I did not place myself around anyone that smoked or drank for the health of my son. I juiced carrots, and of course ate a lot. After his birth, I looked at him and knew I was blessed. I remember, he never cried during the night for his bottle. He would just quietly play with his toys. His smile and his eyes, has always been as bright as the sun. Being married, having my beautiful child was the means of why I stopped going out.

Though I was not attending church at that time, my son was blessed by the pastor in his Christenings Ceremony. Not realizing God was calling me back to Him slowly, even while I was at the church for my son's Christening Ceremony. The enemy on the other hand also knew this. Problems started in my marriage. Not soon after that, my husband and I separated and then divorced. I moved my son and me into an apartment. I began dating a man my age, from Egypt. I truly loved him, more than anyone I had ever dated, (outside of my relationship in boarding school) due to unfortunate circumstances on his behalf, we were separated. I began going out again to clubs on the weekends.

My sister and I would go out a few times on the weekend. I remember one night, we were at a club, and there was a guy trying to talk to my sister, and she was not interested. He kept repeatedly asking for her number, and she replied, by saying, "Not at this time!" In defense of my sister, I do not know what made me say this, but in humor, I said with a very deep voice, "This is my woman!" He walked away in surprise. My purpose was to remove him from making my sister feel uncomfortable. Of course all of this was somewhat humorous to my sister and me. I looked over and the guy was looking at me pointing with his friends. They began spreading to everyone at the club, that I was a man dressed as woman. I later went to tell the young men, to forgive me for saying something that was not true; I attempted to explain to him that my sister was kindly saying she was not interested in so many words, and I was watching this happen from a distance, thinking I must move quickly for her protection, I thought this might intimidate him to leave her alone. Though he and his friends listened and smiled, their facial expression had another story.

As untrue and ridiculous as it sounds, living in a small town, the word began to spread among a couple of the places my sister and I would go out to. The enemy had used people to cast rumors while on his playground. Something done for the benefit for my sister became a problem and attack once again on my character. I smile now, that I even let such nonsense affect me then.

I did not realize at the time, that God was starting to move things around. God was calling me back to Him slowly. He continued placing obstacles in my way, so that I would not become so attached to this lifestyle of going out. He did not want me to get too comfortable in my temporary fix. He allowed me to experience the fun I thought I wanted, and soon my tie would be devoted back to Him, where I always belonged.

I was in another relationship with a man, in who was very generous. His generosity combined with what I had already had allow me to have a little more. I had a brand new Cadillac, CTS; flashy rims, fine clothing, love to wear flashy jewelry, diamonds, and purchased all the most expensive things. There was not much that was lacked material wise.

Though I did not go to church, I would send my tithe and stewardship through my mother for her church. Not knowing that God was touching me, drawing me back to Him but not aggressively but in His perfect timing, within that mere act!

After a while of going out, I began to become bored with it. It was like a veil being removed from my eyes slowly. I begin thinking differently, becoming more sensitive to the needs of others. I wanted a change, but did not know what change that was. I did not know even then that my mind frame was changing because God was drawing me back to Him.

New Years Eve, I called my mother and asked her, if she was going to church. She said, "Yes," and at that moment before thinking I said, "I am coming to!" I know she was so surprised, due to her asking so many times in the past. I had no desire then, due to the rumors said in the past. New Years Eve, I met her at church. I felt touched in my spirit while I was there, when God used the pastor to present his sermon. After the service the pastor said to me, "Mia, I am glad to see you here, will you make me a promise? Will you come back next week?" I said yes to him, but had no attention on coming back. All that week, there was a replay in my mind of the pastor asking me to promise I would return, I thought to myself for a second, if I go back, I might have to give up my freedom, going out from time to time. My life was good so I thought, my son having the things he desired as well as myself. No threatening situations.

Now I can say, that, at that time, I thought my life was good, the material things I had attained was what God opened His hand and gave to me. And as far as "No threatening situations," I thank Him that He protected me from any unseen dangers, I had no knowledge of.

I kept my promise to the pastor, and returned the next week to church, this time during the service, I was so moved, I began to cry. After service, the pastor asked me again, would I promise to come again next week, and and I, quickly this time, without hesitation, said "Yes!" During that week, I felt a strong moving of God's Spirit pulling me to start a new beginning.

I begin going to church every week. This bond that was being built with God, I had never had it before when I was forced to go to church as a child. This bond, made me feel complete. Though I never used drugs, outside of smoking cigarettes, God was becoming a drug to me that I could not get enough of. Each time, I thought of Him, I began to cry, and hurt that I had ever left Him, but thanked Him for my son, and all that He done in protecting us from the enemy, when I was on his turf. My heart was so open, vulnerable and sensitive to others. I was scheduled to be baptized. The day before baptism, I received a call from the church's secretary that baptism was going to have to be rescheduled for a couple of weeks, due to one of the pipes bursting and it not being any hot water. The enemy had tried to discourage me that whole week that my life would change, and be very boring, etc. After a short thought and then decision, I decided to proceed forward with the baptism in spite of the water being cold.

I was baptized, and everyone scheduled to be baptized for that week. I had no desire of going out, drinking or smoke any cigarettes. There was worship in my home every night with such strong power in God's spirit. I had discussed with my boyfriend that I dated before coming to Christ, that I could no longer go out and we could no longer have relations together. After a while, though he cared, decided to no longer fashion me with all the financial means he was giving as before. Finding a new life with God, those things did not longer matter to me.

My fancy car, in which I loved so much, I could no longer keep, due to all my expenses changing. That life of never having to worry about money was now becoming a somewhat small issue. I had to down grade to 1995 Oldsmobile Cutlass. I paid my tithe religiously, and would give most of what I had to the church as a token to God for His goodness, even when bills were at stake. God never failed, though I did not have as much as I did before, there was no lack in my supply. I knew the time would come when I would have triple of what I had before, through God's blessings.

The enemy began to put in my mind, that when I lived a life separate from God, that I had more, and now that I was living for God, I had much less. But I quickly rejected those feelings with looking at the wealth I had in front of me, my child.

Though baptized and a member of the church, I was never offered bible studies through the church. This is important in the nurturing and growth process for new believers. I would have bible studies at home. I must say, things that I have learned were through experience and reading of God's word and continuous prayer.

Each week that the pastor would ask if someone would come to God, and give their life to Him. The thought of the pastor continuously asking, "Is there one soul that will come? God is calling" . . . Being so overjoyed to be a part of His family; I felt continuously that I owed Him. To not move on that request, to sit in my seat, while the pastor is continuously asking anyone to come . . . well, I would go up to the front. Many gossiped that I felt I was so dirty, that was the reason, I kept coming to the front, but God knew my heart. The things that I did for Christ did not make sense to those that were judging, but then it was not for them to understand, only God!

This is a problem in the church today. Many people that leave the church, and then returned are looked at as if they have been tainted of the world. This is the way, I was made to feel. And how could one ever be clean enough to join or rejoin God's family.

The true question is how can anyone born in sin, ever be worthy of the Gift that God gave all mankind, in love, His Son. It is a good thing that God does not look at us, as we look at one another.

I was in the basement, giving my son a snack, and one of the ladies said to me, can I ask you a question, and I said "Yes . . ." she then asked, "How do you get your son to act in such a good manner?" Taken back that she would even ask such a question, I replied by saying, "This is his nature, and it is nourished when we have worship and prayer each night." She had asked me before what my life was like being in the world . . . after answering her, she then decided to ask me how my son acted in such a good manner…I tried to think positively, but I knew where she was going with her questioning, and I quickly ignored it with a smile!

Though many tested my character through rumors, or confronting me with someone else's gossip, I tried my best to reply with a smile. Though I am outspoken, I felt that it was best to keep quiet and not react to any rumors that were said about me through resorting in how the enemy wanted me to act.

After a while of attending church, the feelings of gossip and rumor that made me leave the church in my younger years had begun to scratch at my spirit. I would retract my thinking. I would remind myself that I went to church to honor God, and because I felt it was something I was supposed to do.

The church had a variety of cliques, even the youth, had cliques. Though God cushioned me to not hear all the things that were said about me, the looks given by those claiming to follow Christ were harsher than words. These feelings of ridicule I faced in high school, then in the secular world, were coming forth in the place where I thought my healing would be nourished.

There were all types of things being said, concerning what they thought was in my past. This was the whole problem, it was what they thought, what was discussed, what was gossiped about. Women grasping tight to their husbands, it hurt, how they could of have thought that I would do this, these things I never did when I had left the church. Not looking through God's Eyes, only looking at me through the eyes of someone else. I was called everything but, who I am, a child of God.

My son was not always invited to other children homes for dinner, not because of his character, but the negative thoughts that were felt concerning his mother. We attended church, but did not feel any connection. I know that your focus is to be on God, and not the people, but the things happening and things said were very distracting. Many times I left church crying, instead of the feelings of joy. To those that might be judging at this point, I do understand I should have been stronger, but nurturing from the body of Christ was also needed.

The enemy was not only trying to break my spirit in the church, but soon at the workplace as well. I began working for a assembly plant. Hearing so many past stories about this place, I felt in my spirit, that there could be a potential problem for me; but on the other hand, I was happy to be given the opportunity in making a substantial amount of money. My mother had already shared with me the importance of staying to myself. For this plant is known for heavy gossip, and arguments. And I did just that. When people would speak, I would respond without making a lot of conversation, being friendly due to being the new employee. One instance of gossip; a guy, came to my area at work and in conversation, he pulled out some pictures of a dinner that a few of the workers had attended. On three separate times while showing the picture, he asked if I knew this older guy in the picture. After repeating himself, I asked why he kept asking me did I know this older person, after I had already responded, "No!" He then said, well this older guy has been telling a few people that you went to dinner with him, and that, there was intimacy between you both. In defense of myself, I told him that was not true; I never met this man before.

I then asked if he knew where this person works, so that I may ask why he is saying these things. The man that had showed me the pictures, did not want to be involved, and asked that I not say anything, but I felt like the matter needed to be straightened out. As we are talking this guy just happened to be walking down the aisle where I worked. I asked him did he mind if I talk to him for a moment. He had such a look of guilt. I asked him did he tell anyone that we had been intimate or on a date. He denied saying anything and of course the one that provided the rumor, said, he was only repeating what was told to him . . . at that point, I made it clear in front of both of them, by saying, "So you are admitting the truth that nothing ever happened between us?" He responded by saying, "No, nothing happen!" The next day there was a rumor that I had asked both of the men, I confronted on a date. Other rumors began to surface to disfigure my character. The enemy had spun my character, disfigured my name so badly, that this battle, I could not try to fight. I kept relying on God to speak on my behalf.

As time was passing, it just happen those employees that I worked with, had family members that assisted in spreading rumors to those that went to the same church I attended. There were already rumors disfiguring my character, adding fuel that I was being intimate with men on the job, was more ammunition for words of gossip against me. I felt that if I had of spoken in defense, it would have appeared that it was true, so used to ignoring things people said against me, I just talked to God, and asked Him to speak up for me; the enemy is attacking me at the church, at work, and I needed Him to straighten these matters out.

Many times people would come in the area I worked, to talk about the problems they were facing, and though I to was facing adversity, I buried my hurt, and desire of needing a listening ear, to help them. I would listen and give encouragement, and later when the opportunity would arise, when they are in conversation with trouble seekers that have passed rumors against myself and others, instead of them speaking in my behalf, they did not. This would have meant standing up, speaking out, separating themselves from the crowd, speaking just one kind word in defense of my character. I had done and would have been more than willing to do this same thing for them! It takes a lot of courage and is more challenging to keep moving forward with the adversity of gossip and without an abundant amount of support, then to move forward with support.

A lot of times there are many people that listen to gossip, that really want to say something in defense of someone's character being attacked, but lack the courage to stand up, most cases they feel this might cost them their status of how they might be perceived. What they do not realize is this would actually allow them to gain the respect of the peers. Providing insight where it is really needed. Most do not realize that this is a problem, until those same ones that they were gossiping with, have now made them the target of gossip.

Each day at work, I would carry this huge bag to work every day, filled with things I did not need. I was only reading one or two of the books; I had no need for carrying twelve. Thinking of those moments now, I realize that symbolized extra burdens I did not need to carry. The heavy bag on a spiritual level was me carrying unnecessary burdens. I would talk to God about it, and instead of leaving it with Him to take care of. I would carry it with me every day. My impatience of wanting Him to move quicker on my behalf only slowed the process, due to me always taking the burdens back with me.

On the weekends I would continue to go to church. I kept holding on to God, even when I felt He was not being represented in the proper manner of His true character by those ones that were gossiping. I met a lot of good people in church, but somehow the enemy wanted to keep reminding me, of those that did not show the character of God.

I was so used to carrying burdens, praying about it, and having the feelings of frustration, till after a period of time, this joy I once felt in God was slowly drifting, and being replaced with deep hurt, anger and bitterness. The enemy was attempting to make me believe that God was not concerned about what concerned me, that He did not care about the rumors, that if I was important to Him, He would speak on my behalf among His other children, because I was His child too. I felt overwhelmed and somewhat burned out, after years of being made one of the targets of gossip and after a few times of confronting a rumor and the persons involved denying what was being said, I thought for my sanity, it would be best to ignore it. I would hear the preacher say in the sermon, when your going through a storm . . . God is with you~ I began to cry for, I felt like I had been in the same storm ever since high school. When is this storm going to end? I must say, God has ended it!

I did not have a mentor at church to talk to about all the burdens I was carrying. I did not have anyone but God, and my son. I cried more than I laughed. Gossip had not just robbed me, but it had also robbed my son of receiving a full 100% of his mother's joy. I asked God for help and guidance. And that He would please not allow my hurt to hurt my son in anyway. He would respond by telling me, He was aware of all these things that were happening, and that He can use anything even gossip, rumors. That He would protect my son and allow his life to be blessed; He also wanted me to keep moving forward and also to forgive! He is giving me beauty for my ashes and this dart I was feeling was actually striking Him. ***Psalms 34:13, "The LORD is nigh unto them that are of a broken heart; and saveth such as be of a contrite spirit."*** I remember sitting in my car on St. Clair of Cleveland, crying, and I saw a man walking toward the car, as he walked passed, I said with eyes full of tears and a contrite heart, "I am sorry sir, I do not have money with me to help you right now." This angel dressed in homeless clothing said to me, "I do not need your money; I just wanted to let you know that there are better days ahead!" God knew I was so overwhelmed by rumors against me on the job, rumors against me at church and sent me encouragement, in a unexpected package.

Psalms 34:13, "The LORD is nigh unto them that are of a broken heart; and saveth such as be of a contrite spirit."

Feeling bitter, the enemy had used some, that say they are followers of Christ, to spread rumors, that were untruth and very hurtful so badly, that I begin to question God. I asked God, "If I am Yours, Father, and You love me and died for me, then why aren't You telling the rest of Your children about me? Why are You letting them spread untruth, that would push me away from You? God would remind in my spirit that, *"First of all, this is the enemy at work, to attempt to separate you from Me, My child! I love you, and what others say against you, do not worry, for they are saying it against Me! Keep moving forward, these things are not surprising to Me, but I will use them for My better Glory! Do not worry about what others say about you, for I live inside of you, and I know who you are, and most of all, in Whom you belong to, that is Me, Your Father!"* He also reminded me that there was a purpose that He named me, Mia, for its meaning by Him, means, "Mine!" He said that I am His, He loves me, and does not like in anyway, anyone disfiguring my character, for what they say about me, they are actually saying about Him! That when I pray about someone that has hurt me, He talks to them in many ways, like: in their sleep, while they are driving, on the job or through a sermon . . . but many times they neglected to listen to His spirit speaking. That He touched their heart and spoke to their spirit that their participation in gossip was wrong, but they ignored what was told to them. But those that truly feared and loved the Lord, were listening and making immediate changes, and that He would introduce them to me. My Father was taking care of matters, just as He said He would! He would also repay me for the gossip I had endured for Him!

Though God always reminded me of His love, and His awareness of what had happened, on some occasions, I felt bound by feelings of bitterness, and so much gossip unresolved, confrontation, no one admitting their part in gossip; I felt it best to keep silent and stay calm. It was not that I was afraid, but more afraid of what I might say as a result of experiencing it over a period of time. Confronting the accuser seemed to be a dead end, each time those involved denying the damage they had created. I realized that how could I confront an accuser of gossip, when the true accuser of gossip was the enemy. How could I fight rumors that for years, I had been quiet about, I felt where would I begin. For years my once out going spirit, full of laughter and love for life, before I came to God, was now just a distant memory. The worst feeling was that the matters of gossip imposed on my character, had not been resolved. I had great depression, unhappiness and discomfort for many years. Though I was still functional, I knew the change. And most of all, my son recognized the change. I continued to talk to God about it. I said, Lord, I did not inflict these wounds myself, but they were inflicted by some of those that are followers of You, and others that were not yet followers of You, but thank you Father, for I know You are working on it. I can say God has and is resolving the matters of gossip that had affected me!

Through battling forgiveness in my heart for those that had cast rumors, I asked God, please to help me forgive, to not allow me to stay in the pit of depression or anger toward those that had spoken evil against me. I found myself saying, "No weapon formed . . . even when I did not fully understand the direction a conversation was going, when talking with someone. I saw so many followers of Christ happy to be a part God's family, but somehow I was not feeling it as much, I felt I was robbed of that joy, through the gossip of others misrepresenting God.

Even though God had constantly confirmed to me, whom I was in Him, and reminded that He was not in any way ignorant to what was happening. The enemy attempted to use these inner feelings, I once was so good at hiding from others out of protection to me, to resurface. The enemy gossiped to my mind that, God saw what was happening, and that I was not important to Him, as He had told me I was, that some thought I was afraid to speak up for myself, and thought that I was weak, due to me not responding to the many accusations and rumors that had been spread. That God could not use me, because I was so damaged. These feelings only added to my hurt, and led to me believing that my hope of one day being cleared of whom I was striving to become in God, would never take place. Once again, I can say God has and is resolving the matters of gossip that had affected me!

Due to these feelings, I felt I had to show a more aggressive attitude by defending myself. I began at times having an attitude in the way I talked, when talking to someone as my defense mechanism. I felt it was most important to not show any weaknesses when talking to someone. So when I would speak, most would consider it aggressive, but it was me lashing out inwardly, by saying why you are gossiping about me, why are you judging me, why are you allowing the enemy to use you like this? In protection of myself, I could not say what I was feeling inwardly, outwardly in words, so I lashed out in retaliation of my feelings. I do understand that this was wrong, but it was also wrong to be prejudged and placed in a position of having to feel this way by those misjudging and casting rumors. It is expected of the world, but not expected from the hospital, which on a spiritual level is the church body of Christ.

Even through my feelings of bitterness and hurt, it never affected my desire of giving to the church, my faithfulness in tithe and stewardship and helping those in need. It was the enemy's hope that I would resent people so much that, I would not want to help anyone in need or continue to give God, what is rightfully His. Even after the pressures of not feeling completely comforted and apart of the body of Christ. I maintained home, planned various things for my son, weekends was ours to go dinner or any fun activity. Each year we would go on cruises wherever he chooses. Our businesses have been prospering and growing! I was functional in spite of my hurt. I would again continue to pray and ask God that He would not allow my hurt, inflicted by the enemy through others, to harm the precious gift He had given me, my son. My son has always been well taken care of; there were not too many material things that I did not provide for him through God. God blessed me financially to make all these things possible. He has all the latest gadgets, clothing and much more, I provided him with a lot of things he needed and wanted to compensate in my mind, for my discreet depression. We prayed in worship each night, and I would always share with him that he would be better than me in every way and that his life is and always will be blessed, without pain and sorrow. The seeds of giving I have continuously planted into God' Kingdom will benefit greatly for him and me as well, without pain and sorrow.

Unfortunately, after many years of going through the pain of gossip and being misunderstood, I stop going to church. Though I knew I needed to keep going for the spiritual enhancement of my son. Knowing that I had more tears from hurt of those that had gossip against me, and felt less encouraged, than being encouraged. For my sanity, I left. My once good image of many of those in the church was now exchange with feelings of hypocrisy and wanting to know what the purpose of the body of Christ was there for. I would even drop my son off at church at times, and I would go home and read my bible, to avoid being around those that had gossiped. Now there were few that did not participate in such actions of gossip, but since I never shared my feelings of what happened, their "hello's and God bless you" was not enough at the time to soothe my wounds, all of course apart of the plan of the enemy.

There are a lot of good people that are still following God that are not in the church, due to be being wounded by gossip in the body of Christ. It is most challenging to follow God without acceptance and support of those claiming to follow God, than it is for person (s) within the church that are receiving support and acceptance within the church's body. And for this I know why God has allowed this book to come forth, to speak out concerning matters that are a concern for Him. This concern has lasted for centuries, much too long. The hospital; the church is full of a variety of sicknesses, which symbolizes the church body of Christ and it's variety of circumstances deeming to need His help and guidance. This body needs to produce more support and acceptance into God's family. And to rid the gossip, lack of support, lack of acceptance and judgmental attitudes out of His family, for this is not His actions and not His character.

I look now on these things that had happened and can clearly see the fingerprints of the enemy all over the situations that had taken place in the past. It has taken me a long time to forgive and move forward. Each day my hurt is being removed, and as a result through this book. Writing this book is finally gives me the chance to explain how I have felt for many years, and to provide the truth of my story and the problems I was affected by through gossip. My testimony of still holding on to God, even though He had been misrepresented, will give encouragement to so many that have been affected by gossip, and will enlighten those that participate in gossip of where gossip has stemmed from; the enemy.

Throughout all my experiences of gossip, I realized that I kept asking God for something that He had already given me, a testimony! I did not have an earthly mentor that I could share my pain with, but I have always had God. My healing and therapy came when I began expressing feelings that I attempted to bury. These thoughts in this book exemplify what I had and others like me are looking for, what is needed and most of all what needs to be removed in the church, at the workplace, youth in the schools, marriages, those in magazines or tabloids and most of all our communities; each looking for a chance at sharing the other side to the story, their story; this truth that no one knows but God and them. For many years, I felt that the gossip would just go away, eventually. God in all His Greatness knew better. He knew not only would I receive my healing through writing this book, but it would also provide great comfort to so many others that also feel the same way I do.

Am I healed? I answer "Yes! Through God, He has and will continue to multiply the beauty for my scarred heart" Yesterday weapon formed against me, shall not prosper today and anymore after that. Jesus has said with *"His stripes, I am healed."* I can say truly now that God has finally spoken in my behalf, through this book; for this knowledge shared was only through His wisdom. As much as I would love to take the credit, I could not, for this knowledge I could not have obtained on my own, only through God's wisdom, spirited through the writings in this book. And as an added bonus, He kept His promise of blessing my son's life; He has placed a very powerful and beautiful cover over him. My son is my successor in anything he decides to do in God's Name, it will be blessed, and without pain and sorrow, and my restoration is completed with a bonus of God sending Christian friends that are not perfect, but that are attempting to represent His character, and practices not participating in gossip. Every business I desired to establish, God granted it to me with favor! I am very excited for all of God's promises of blessings that have unraveled! For all of this and the many blessings to come, I am grateful.

In Closing

It is our Creator's desire to increase His family with individuals with a variety of hurts, sicknesses and spiritual gifts, each showing the wounds and deliverance through testimony for the growth of the next one coming along. For this is why, in creating mankind, God made us with such variety of colors, personalities, languages and special gifts, for each testimony to be shared, nurtured and loved to re-create to continue in harmony.

It is the enemies desire to decrease the body of Christ, for this is less souls that he would have to burn for. The method the enemy attempts to use, is the same method he has always used from the beginning of time, through attempting to turn mankind against one another, especially the members of the body of Christ. The main tool he attempts over and over again is through gossip, non support, non acceptance and judgmental attitudes of one another. The enemy must think mankind are so ignorant, and are not able to catch on to his tactics. This deceiver, liar and hater of all mankind, knows that once we were to join together to work with one another, instead of his plan of working against one another, that he would lose all holds and powers he desires so much to have over mankind, and especially the body of Christ as a whole.

Followers of God are anointed and appointed for particular purposes. This purpose is not to abuse those within and those to come. God commands that those that follow Him do not abuse the power and position as God's anointed. God does not want anyone in the body of Christ or out, to touch His anointed ones, and to cause any harm to His prophets, for God has rebuked even kings that have gotten in the way of His chosen ones. With this being said, since God is the Only One that knows and uses people, no one can judge each member in the body of Christ's position with God, due to their mistakes or past. God is the judge, the Protector and most of all, our inside God. Judging circumstances, pointing the finger is the tool, the enemy uses against mankind daily in complaint to God, to have his way, to destroy mankind.

I have seen that there are many Christians that have come to Christ and many that wanted to come to Christ, that have been hurt by the enemy through others. Not recognizing that the enemy is the culprit of any and all pain, many have left the church, believing that they could not be used by God, or that they could never be welcomed in God's family, due to their pass. The enemy, the accuser of all brethren, used others to make them feel that the road that their traveling on was not worth it and too complicated to think of completing. Many had the feelings of wanting to give up, or just gave up. I can only say these things from how I felt. ***The enemy wanted me to be silenced, so that he could not be exposed of whom he really is, and that is the true perpetrator of gossip.*** This will shine light where he attempted to cast darkness. But I speak in their defense and mine right now, by saying! **"NO WEAPON FORMED AGAINST YOU OR I SHALL PROSPER, IN JESUS NAME!"**

I will not be quiet anymore. God does not create junk, and my life has a purpose, despite what others wanted me to believe or attempted to lead me to believe through the spread of rumors. I will not be depressed anymore, I will smile, because life is good, but God has been greater in more ways than one. It has taken me along time to realize that my existence was perfected by God, and my position in Him will not be moved, and most of all, that God loves me and what I thought was my hurtful concern, was actually God's hurtful concerns from the beginning unfolding.

Many churches pray to God, to increase their church and body of Christ within their church, but in God's eyes there is no separation of churches, but only one body in Him. With this request they fell to understand their request, for Whom in love, has many children of variety, and is more than willing to fulfill such a request. But His concerns of gossip in the body of Him, is something that He really wants to be looked into and then eliminated, before He can increase the churches request as He truly desires.

The enemy has hurt so many people in so many different ways, and there is a lack of support, lack of acceptance and judgmental attitudes in the churches that are looking to receive increases, but some are not ready; how can those really hurt, be received or better yet understood? If those already apart of the body of Christ are rejected, how can new members needing to come that have serious hurts not visible to the non-eye of God, be received in a loving way, most of all looked at through the Eyes of God.

I truly pray that many that read this book will be touched in their spirit of the many changes that need to occur now, for the benefit of all! Most of all that those that have already come to God, will see those that are looking for a family, those looking to become a part of God's family, and those already a part of the body of Christ, through no longer their own eyes, but through God's loving Eyes. This very task right away will defeat the enemy, and defeat his purpose of separation of mankind through gossip!

"Things Impossible For Man, Are and Will Be Possible For God!"

I ask once more, "Now that you know where gossip has stemmed from, and it affects, will you now **STOP THE GOSSIPING?**"

"Lord Increase Our Church"

Article By: Mia F. Stubbs

In God's dwelling, the pastor and the church are praying for increase. God says, "The Harvest is plenty and the laborers are few."

In church service, one morning a prostitute and a drug dealer, dressed not up to the standards of those that are judging, walks in the door. They are gossiped and rejected by the members of God's dwelling; they leave, never to return to that church.

Next week church service, the pastor and the church prays again for increase for the church.

God responds by showing, He sent the increase through the prostitute and drug dealer. God was going to increase the church through them. Through the prostitute and drug dealer, He was going to bring thousands off the streets that are lost.

God is a mysterious God, He sends unexpected packages to accomplish His Greatest Tasks . . . so that then He Will Be Glorified!

Facing Your Inner Silence . . .

Author By: Mia F. Stubbs

How do you explain your inner silence to those that are observing you? Not knowing how to express your feelings within, can push to silence and withdrawal, leaving the assumption to others that your present circumstances are a result of punishment from life, previous things you've done. In some cases that can be true, but in other cases, it can be a means of learning how to reach out to others that are experiencing it too, that has not tapped into their inner strength. Your unwarranted circumstances becomes a mediator for a person in a similar situation that is facing indescribable adversity~

Our circumstances never define us, only our strength!

Perky? No Hurt! . . . .

Author By: Mia F. Stubbs

Not being perky does not mean your depressed . . . Your hurt does not allow you to access a perky personality that you had before your hurt was inflicted.

Our adversity on a higher scale was not aimed for us really . . . Our adversity orchestrated by the enemy was actually aimed to shoot God, but since we are His creations, we are caught in the cross fire.

God in return says, since you were hit for me, I will use it to bless you and bless your seed, and you will be able to bring others that have experienced this same shot from the enemy out with you . . .

And Uhhh, My child, do not worry about your perkiness! I will restore it three fold!

No Man Is An Island . . .

Author By: Mia F. Stubbs

Though our circumstances may make us want to be invisible. God has created this whole entire earth, from planet to animal to human being. Each having its own purpose, to work toward a planned operation. God works through and by no other way but order. Each ordered step given to man by God, are to assist in the deliverance of the person, we are designed to help. We cannot deliver ourselves from our own circumstance, but through moving without delay to help the next one waiting to be delivered, we in return are favorably delivered by God, out of our own circumstances.

God is a Spirit, He uses His creations to show His Love, Greatness, Power, Forgiveness and Mercy!

Sharing Our Experience . . .

Articles By: Mia F. Stubbs

Sharing our experience does not set us aside from the rest, but allows others to have the freedom to dissect various parts of the issue they can relate to. We must remember what we have and are experiencing has happen to the one before us and before them as well. Just as the world goes round and round, so has lack of communication and experience of each other that keeps causing reoccurrence of pain.

The good thing is, just as the world goes round, change can happen to be passed down from generation to generation, a new era of communication openly, peace and a whole lot of joy.

In Dedication of Our World

I believe there will be an appointed day, a National Holiday called, **"Stop The Gossiping Day"** where no one is to gossip for that day . . . until gossip has completely ended!

A day of freedom from the harassment of gossip. A day of peace and togetherness and a day where everyone speaks words of power and strength for one another.

These things impossible for man, **Are Possible For God!**

Share Your Personal Notes Of Victory For This Year?

www.ingramcontent.com/pod-product-compliance
Lightning Source LLC
Chambersburg PA
CBHW031241280526
45784CB00004B/1667